HIPPOCRENE

TWI BASIC COURSE

J.E. Redden
N. Owusu

HIPPOCRENE BOOKS
New York

First published by the Foreign Service Institute, U.S. Government Printing Office, 1963.

Hippocrene paperback edition, 1995.

For information, address:
HIPPOCRENE BOOKS, INC.
171 Madison Avenue
New York, NY 10016

ISBN 0-7818-0394-2

Printed in the United States of America.

TABLE OF CONTENTS

Introduction

Twi is spoken in the southern two-thirds of Ghana, mainly between the Volta and Tano Rivers, but in the last few centuries it has spread over a larger area, especially to the west, so that there are now a large number of speakers in contiguous areas. There are about three million native speakers of Twi, plus about one million more persons who regularly use the language. All dialects of Twi are mutually intelligible; but at conversational speed and on some subjects, speakers from distant areas may have difficulty understanding one another.

The first grammar of Twi was published in Copenhagen in 1764. Missionaries began to publish in Twi in the second quarter of the nineteenth century. Akuapim Twi, spoken in the south-east was the first dialect used for Bible translation and other literature. Because of this, Akuapim Twi became the prestige dialect and is still regarded by many people as the 'real' or 'pure' Twi. Fanti Twi, spoken in the south-central area, is rather different from the other dialects and also has a fairly extensive literature. This manual uses Ashanti Twi, spoken in the central area and by far the largest dialect. The speaker on whose speech the materials are based is from the eastern part of the Ashanti area, and some differences will be noted between the speech of Kumasi, regarded as the standard, and the form used herein. An effort has been made in the footnotes to indicate such differences.

There is also the tendency to use the name of the local dialect as a name of the language, e.g., Ashanti instead of Ashanti Twi. Often Akuapim Twi and Twi are used interchangeably, a practice which speakers of other forms of Twi don't always appreciate. Because of this, an attempt is being made to substitute the name Akan for Twi. Akan is an ethnographic term referring to all the peoples of the area and consequently is not felt to favor any one group or form of the language above the others.

The Bureau of Ghana Languages has developed a common script
for all the Twi dialects. The transcription system used in this
manual is the standard orthography plus a number of diacritic
markings to indicate tone, which is not usually written, and to
make it clear how a word or segment is pronounced in cases where
the student may have difficulty in interpreting the orthography.
Some words have been respelled; but to indicate this, the mark °
is placed before a respelled word the first time it occurs, and
the regular spelling is given in a footnote. English words, which
are very commonly used even when speaking about everyday affairs,
have been respelled as they are pronounced in Twi unless the word
is one where an attempt would be made to pronounce it in the
English fashion, e.g. /univérsity/, but /sirèn̩/, 'shilling'.

Twi, like almost all the languages spoken south of the Sahara,
is a tone language. Each syllable has its own tone or pitch.
It is just as important to get the correct tones as it is to get
the correct vowels and consonants. There are many words that are
distinguished only by their tones, e.g., /papa/ 'a palm-leaf fan'
(with two low tones), /pápa/, 'good' (with two high tones), and
/papá/, 'father' (with a low followed by a high tone).

Twi has three contrastive or phonemic tones: high /´/
mid /ˈ/
low /ˇ/
Like many West African tone systems, Twi tones are terraced, i.e.,
mid tone is always a downstep in absolute pitch from the preceding
syllable, and there is no upstep in the sequence mid to high, but
the pitch remains approximately the same. After a low tone there
are two possibilities: (1) remain on approximately the same pitch,
which is interpreted as low, and (2) step up to a higher level,
which is interpreted as high. After a juncture, i.e., a pause,
there are also only two possibilities: (1) high, or (2) low.
After a high or a mid tone, there are three possibilities (1)
remain on approximately the same pitch, which is interpreted as

high; (2) step down slightly, which is interpreted as mid, and
(3) step down a greater amount, which is interpreted as low.

After reaching the most prominent syllable of the sentence,
usually the first high tone, the pitch level of the whole sentence
gradually steps down so that a high near the end of the sentence
may be lower than a low near the beginning of the sentence. A
prominent syllable is usually stressed, i.e., louder than sur-
rounding syllables

That is to say, on any one syllable in any one position in
the sentence, there are at the most only three possible tones:
high, mid, and low; but the absolute pitch of the syllable is
limited or determined by a number of factors. The first tone in
an utterance is more or less determined by the natural pitch
level of the speaker's voice, and somewhat by his emotions. (See
Unit 5 note 12 for explanation of statement and question intonation.)

Perhaps diagrams will make this clearer.

TONE TERRACING

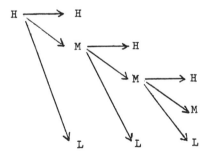

SENTENCE INTONATION

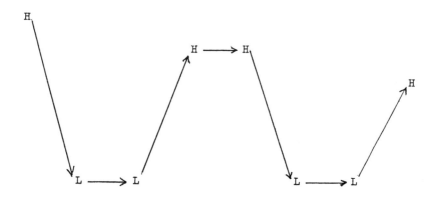

The above diagrams illustrate the pitch level of a sentence being gradually lowered by either tone terracing or sentence intonation; but in a real sentences both of these factors operate simultaneously.

A single low between two highs is higher in pitch than are two or more lows between highs. In addition, the second high of the high-low-high is lower than that of the high-low-low-high sequence. Because of this, the sequences high-low-high and high-mid-high are easily confused by the new student. Using the first two diagrams as source, compare the diagrams below.

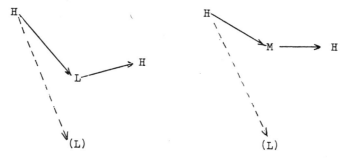

The system for marking tones used in this manual does not mark every syllable. Unmarked initial syllables and unmarked syllables after a low tone are low. Unmarked syllables after a high or mid tone are high. Word boundaries are indicated by spaces between words, and the tone marking system begins anew after each space.

In the five column chart given below, column I gives the symbols used in this manual, column II gives those used by the ordinary orthography, column III gives the phonemes, column IV gives the phonetic symbols, and column V is an approximation of the sound using American English and French sounds for comparison.

I	II	III	IV	V
Symbol	Orthography	Phoneme	Phonetics	Approximation
p	p	/p/	[pʰ]	<u>p</u>in
t	t	/t/	[tʰ, tꞔ][1.]	<u>t</u>in
k	k	/k/	[kʰ]	<u>c</u>ome
ky	ky	/k/	[č][1.]	<u>ch</u>in
b	b	/b/	[b]	<u>b</u>e
d	d	/d/	[d][1.]	<u>d</u>o
g	g	/g/	[g]	<u>g</u>o
gy	gy	/g/	[ǰ][1.]	<u>g</u>em
f	f	/f/	[f]	<u>f</u>ee
s	s	/s/	[s]	<u>s</u>ee
h	h	/h/	[h]	<u>h</u>oe
hy	hy	/h/	[ç][1.]	whispered <u>he</u>
m	m	/m/	[m]	<u>m</u>e
n	n	/n/	[n]	<u>n</u>o
ŋ̣	n	/n/	[ŋ]	si<u>ng</u>
ŋg	ng	/nn/	[ŋŋ]	double ŋ
ñ	n	/n/	[ɲ]	<u>y</u>e pronounced through the nose
ñy	ng	/n/	[ɲ][1.]	ɲ

ñ́ñy	nny	/nn/	[ɲɲ] [1.]	double ɲ
ñ́y	ny	/nn/	[ɲɲ] [1.]	double ɲ
ñg	ng	/n/	[ɲ] [1.]	ɲ
r	r	/r/	[r, ř, ɽ]	t<u>r</u>ee, la<u>dd</u>er
w	w	/w/	[w]	<u>w</u>ant
w̌	w	/w/	[ɥ] [1.]	French lu<u>i</u>
tw	tw	/kʷ/	[č ɥ] [1.]	simultaneous <u>ch</u>ew and w̌
dw	dw	/gʷ/	[ǰ ɥ] [1.]	simultaneous <u>j</u>ump and w̌
ḍw	dw	/g/	[ǰ]	simultaneous <u>j</u>ump and w
gu	gu	/gʷ/[1.], /gu/	[ǰ ɥ] [2.]	Cf. dw
hw	hw	/hʷ/	[h ɥ]	simultaneous ç and <u>wh</u>en
ŋw	nw	/nw/	[ŋʊ ʷ]	ŋ plus rounded ŋ
ñw̌	nw	/nnʷ/	[ɲɲ ɥ]	ɲ plus rounded ɲ
ñ́ʊ̃	nu	/nʷɪ̃/	[ɲ ɥ ɪ̃]	rounded ɲ plus nasalized ɪ
ŋ̣h	nh	/nh/	[ŋŋ̥]	ŋ plus ŋ without voice hum
l	l	/l/ [3.]	[l, r, rʷ, d]	he<u>ll</u>o
v	v	/v/ [3.]	[v, f, b]	a<u>v</u>enue
ɪ	ɪ	/ɪ/	[ɪ̂]	b<u>ea</u>t[5]
ẹ	e	/ɪ/, /e/[4.]	[ɪ̂]	b<u>i</u>t
e	e	/e/	[ě]	b<u>ai</u>t[5]
ɛ	ɛ	/ɛ/	[ɛ]	b<u>e</u>t
ạ	a	/əe/, /a/[4]	[æ]	b<u>a</u>t
a	a	/a/	[a]	b<u>o</u>ttle

ɔ	ɔ	/ɔ/	[ɔ]	b<u>ou</u>ght
o	o	/o/	[oˆ]	b<u>oa</u>t[5]
ọ	o	/u/, /o/[4]	[Uˆ]	b<u>oo</u>k
u	u	/u/	[uˆ]	b<u>oo</u>t[5]
ĩ	ı,ĩ[6·]	/ĩ/	[ĩ~]	nasalized ı
ẽ	e,ẽ[4·]	/ĩ/	[ĩˆ]	nasalized I
ɛ̃	ɛ,ɛ̃[4·]	/ɛ̃/	[ɛ̃ˆ]	nasalized ɛ
ą̃	a,ą̃	/æ̃/	[æˆ]	nasalized æ
ã	a,ã	/ã/	[ã]	nasalized a
ɔ̃	ɔ,ɔ̃[4·]	/ɔ̃/	[ɔ̃]	nasalized ɔ
õ	o,õ[4·]	/ũ/	[ũˆ]	nasalized u
ũ	u,ũ	/ũ/	[ũˆ]	nasalized u

.	.	/#/	step down in pitch on pre-ceeding syllable and pause
,	,	/ | /	pause and/or step down in pitch on the following syllable
?	?	/ || /	elevation of the whole sentence level and a steep, abrupt fall on preceding syllable.
!	!	/X/	preceding syllable at least tripled in length

A number of special symbols are also used as explained below.

( ) Enclosed Twı elements usually elided at conversation speed.

(ꞌ ꞌ) Literal English translation of the Twı.

/ / In the chart above, this symbol, means Twi phonemics;
elsewhere, when enclosing Twi, it means the symbolization used
in this grammar. When enclosing English, it means words not
occurring in the Twi, but needed for clarity or accuracy of translation in English.

// // Standard Twi orthography. Spaces between words to mark
word boundaries are the same as those used in the orthography
except as given in the footnotes.

NOTES

1. In general, before front vowels all consonants are to a
greater or lesser degree palatalized and stops affricated, but
the exact distribution of allophones, especially of /n/, is
quite complex.

2. In Ashanti /gu/ when followed by a vowel is pronounced like
/dw/; but in Akuapim and some other dialects, it is still pronounced /gu/.

3. /l/ and /v/ are used in recent loan-words only.

4. In most dialects there is little or no contrast of /ẹ/ versus
/e/, /ọ/ versus /o/, /ạ/ versus /a/, /ẽ/ versus /ɛ/, and /õ/
versus /ɔ/.

5. There is no y- or w- offglide with Twi vowels in contrast to
English vowels which sound somewhat the same.

6. Nasalized vowels are regularly indicated in the transcription.
The ordinary orthography does not usually mark nasalized vowels.
Where there is ambiguity, the nasalized vowel is sometimes marked.
In the transcription, only the first vowel of a cluster of nasal-
ized vowels is marked with /~/.

Unit I

Unit I consists of forty-eight drills of pairs of words
that are distinguished by tone or consonant and vowel differences that often cause difficulty for speakers of English.
On the tapes at the beginning of each drill, the two words
are translated, identified as to how they differ, and said
twice. Each drill is divided into two parts. In the first
part, ten pairs of words are given. The student is to listen
to the pairs and to tell whether the two words are <u>same</u> or
<u>different</u>. Space is left on the tapes so that the student
will have time to answer before the correct answer is given
for verification. In the second part, ten single words are
given. The student is to identify each word by its <u>distinc-
tive</u> <u>difference</u> as explained at the beginning of each drill.
Again space is left on the tape for the student to answer
before verification is given.

Drill 1 - tones

he opens, low low high, ɔbaá
a woman, low high high, ɔbáa

1.	ɔbáa	lhh
2.	ɔbaá	llh
3.	ɔbáa	lhh
4.	ɔbaá	llh
5.	ɔbaá	llh
6.	ɔbáa	lhh
7.	ɔbáa	lhh
8.	ɔbáa	lhh
9.	ɔbaá	llh
10.	ɔbaá	llh

Drill 2 - vowel length

a child, short, ɔbá
a woman, long, ɔbáa

1.	ɔbá	s
2.	ɔbáa	l
3.	ɔbáa	l
4.	ɔbáa	l
5.	ɔbá	s
6.	ɔbáa	l
7.	ɔbá	s
8.	ɔbáa	l
9.	ɔbá	s
10.	ɔbá	s

Drill 3 - tones

entirely, hhh, kǫraa
small calabash, llh, kǫraá

1.	kǫraa	hhh
2.	kǫraá	llh
3.	kǫraa	hhh
4.	kǫraá	llh
5.	kǫraa	hhh
6.	kǫraa	hhh
7.	kǫraá	llh
8.	kǫraá	llh
9.	kǫraa	hhh
10.	kǫraá	llh

Drill 4 - tones

brother-in-law, lllh, akóntá
arithmetic, lhmlh akóntàá

1.	akóntá	lllh
2.	akóntàá	lhmlh
3.	akóntá	lllh
4.	akóntá	lllh
5.	akóntàá	lhmlh
6.	akóntàá	lhmlh
7.	akóntá	lllh
8.	akóntá	lllh
9.	akóntàá	lhmlh
10.	akóntá	lllh

2

Drill 5 - tones

good, high high, pápa
father, low high, papá

1.	pápa	hh
2.	papá	lh
3.	papá	lh
4.	pápa	hh
5.	papá	lh
6.	pápa	hh
7.	papá	lh
8.	pápa	hh
9.	papá	lh
10.	pápa	hh

Drill 6 - tones

a fan, low low, papa
good, high high, pápa

1.	papa	ll
2.	pápa	hh
3.	pápa	hh
4.	papa	ll
5.	pápa	hh
6.	papa	ll
7.	papa	ll
8.	pápa	hh
9.	papa	ll
10.	pápa	hh

Drill 7 - tones

a fan, low low, papa
father, low high, papá

1.	papa	ll
2.	papá	lh
3.	papá	lh
4.	papa	ll
5.	papá	lh
6.	papá	lh
7.	papa	ll
8.	papa	ll
9.	papá	lh
10.	papa	ll

Drill 8   vowel length

a fan, short, papa
to pat, long, paapaa

1.	papa	s
2.	paapaa	l
3.	paapaa	l
4.	papa	s
5.	paapaa	l
6.	papa	s
7.	papa	s
8.	paapaa	l
9.	papa	s
10.	paapaa	l

Drill 9 - tones and length

male twin, low high, atá
female twin, low low high, ataá

1.	atá	lh
2.	ataá	llh
3.	atá	lh
4.	ataá	llh
5.	ataá	llh
6.	atá	lh
7.	atá	lh
8.	ataá	llh
9.	atá	lh
10.	ataá	llh

Drill 10 - tones

to speak, low low, kasa
a language, high mid, kásá

1.	kásá	hm
2.	kasa	ll
3.	kásá	hm
4.	kásá	hm
5.	kasa	ll
6.	kásá	hm
7.	kásá	hm
8.	kasa	ll
9.	kásá	hm
10.	kásá	hm

Drill 11 - tones

it is different, lll, ɛsɔnɔ
elephant, lhh, ɛsɔ́nɔ

1.	ɛsɔ́nɔ	lhh
2.	ɛsɔnɔ	lll
3.	ɛsɔ́nɔ	lhh
4.	ɛsɔnɔ	lll
5.	ɛsɔ́nɔ	lhh
6.	ɛsɔ́nɔ	lhh
7.	ɛsɔnɔ	lll
8.	ɛsɔnɔ	lll
9.	ɛsɔ́nɔ	lhh
10.	ɛsɔnɔ	lll

Drill 12 - tones

to hold, seize, low low, fuą
single, one, low high, fuą́

1.	fuą	ll
2.	fuą́	lh
3.	fuą́	lh
4.	fuą	ll
5.	fuą	ll
6.	fuą́	lh
7.	fuą	ll
8.	fuą́	lh
9.	fuą́	lh
10.	fuą́	lh

Drill 13 - tones

white, high high high, fúfuo
fufu, low high high, fufúo

1.	fúfuo	hhh
2.	fúfuo	hhh
3.	fufúo	lhh
4.	fúfuo	hhh
5.	fufúo	lhh
6.	fufúo	lhh
7.	fúfuo	hhh
8.	fufúo	lhh
9.	fufúo	lhh
10.	fúfuo	hhh

Drill 14 - tones

to tell a lie, low high, bǫá
to help, low low, bǫa

1.	bǫa	ll
2.	bǫa	ll
3.	bǫá	lh
4.	bǫa	ll
5.	bǫá	lh
6.	bǫá	lh
7.	bǫa	ll
8.	bǫá	lh
9.	bǫá	lh
10.	bǫa	ll

Drill 15 - vowel length

something, long, hwęę
to beat, short, hwę́

1.	hwę́	s
2.	hwę́	s
3.	hwęę	l
4.	hwę́	s
5.	hwęę	l
6.	hwęę	l
7.	hwę́	s
8.	hwęę	l
9.	hwę́	s
10.	hwę́	s

Drill 16 - nasal vowel

to take, oral, fa
to be hoarse, nasal, fã

1.	fa	o
2.	fa	o
3.	fã	n
4.	fã	n
5.	fa	o
6.	fã	n
7.	fa	o
8.	fa	o
9.	fã	n
10.	fã	n

Drill 17 - nasal vowel

hand, oral, nsá
palm wine, nasal, nsá̱

1.	nsá	o
2.	nsá̱	n
3.	nsá̱	n
4.	nsá	o
5.	nsá̱	n
6.	nsá	o
7.	nsá	o
8.	nsá̱	n
9.	nsá	o
10.	nsá	o

Drill 18 - vowel length

to be hoarse, short, fã
tottering, long, fãa

1.	fã	s
2.	fãa	l
3.	fãa	l
4.	fã	s
5.	fã	s
6.	fãa	l
7.	fã	s
8.	fãa	l
9.	fã	s
10.	fã	s

Drill 19 - nasal vowel

to dip, oral, sa
to lie along, nasal, sã

1.	sa	o
2.	sa	o
3.	sã	n
4.	sa	o
5.	sã	n
6.	sã	n
7.	sa	o
8.	sã	n
9.	sã	n
10.	sa	o

Drill 20 - vowel before /r/

to mix, ẹ, fẹ́rà
to put on native dress, u, fura

1.	fẹ́rà	ẹ
2.	fẹ́rà	ẹ
3.	fura	u
4.	fẹ́rà	ẹ
5.	fura	u
6.	fura	u
7.	fẹ́rà	ẹ
8.	fura	u
9.	fẹ́rà	ẹ
10.	fura	u

Drill 21 - tones

to thatch, low low, kuru
a sore, high high, kúru

1.	kuru	ll
2.	kuru	ll
3.	kúru	hh
4.	kuru	ll
5.	kúru	hh
6.	kúru	hh
7.	kuru	ll
8.	kúru	hh
9.	kúru	hh
10.	kuru	ll

Drill 22 - vowel before /r/

to leave, ẹ, kẹ́rà
to grasp, u, kura

1.	kẹ́rà	ẹ
2.	kura	u
3.	kẹ́rà	ẹ
4.	kura	u
5.	kura	u
6.	kẹ́rà	ẹ
7.	kẹ́rà	ẹ
8.	kura	u
9.	kẹ́rà	ẹ
10.	kura	u

Drill 23 - tones

co-wife, high low, kọ́rà
to hide, low low, kọra

1.	kọ́rà	hl
2.	kọ́rà	hl
3.	kọra	ll
4.	kọ́rà	hl
5.	kọra	ll
6.	kọra	ll
7.	kọ́rà	hl
8.	kọra	ll
9.	kọra	ll
10.	kọ́rà	hl

Drill 24 - tones

soul, high mid, kẹ́rà
to leave, high low, kẹ́rà

1.	kẹ́rà	hm
2.	kẹ́rà	hl
3.	kẹ́rà	hl
4.	kẹ́rà	hm
5.	kẹ́rà	hl
6.	kẹ́rà	hm
7.	kẹ́rà	hm
8.	kẹ́rà	hl
9.	kẹ́rà	hm
10.	kẹ́rà	hl

Drill 25 - fricatives

like, as, s, sɛ (alveolar)
insert, hy, hyɛ (palatal)

1.	sɛ	s
2.	sɛ	s
3.	hyɛ	hy
4.	hyɛ	hy
5.	sɛ	s
6.	hyɛ	hy
7.	sɛ	s
8.	hyɛ	hy
9.	hyɛ	hy
10.	sɛ	s

Drill 26 - palatal affricates

to cut up, voiced, dwą
to cut, voiceless, twą

1.	dwą	vd
2.	twą	vl
3.	twą	vl
4.	dwą	vd
5.	twą	vl
6.	dwą	vd
7.	dwą	vd
8.	twą	vl
9.	dwą	vd
10.	dwą	vd

Drill 27 - vowel before /r/

to tie up, bind, ę, dwęrę
to crush, mash, ɛ, dwɛrę

1.	dwęrę	ę
2.	dwęrę	ę
3.	dwɛrę	ɛ
4.	dwɛrę	ɛ
5.	dwęrę	ę
6.	dwɛrę	ɛ
7.	dwęrę	ę
8.	dwɛrę	ɛ
9.	dwɛrę	ɛ
10.	dwęrę	ę

Drill 28 - ñ after nasal vowel

to lie along, without ñ, sã
to return, with ñ, są́ñ

1.	sã	ṽ
2.	są́ñ	ṽñ
3.	sã	ṽ
4.	są́ñ	ṽñ
5.	sã	ṽ
6.	sã	ṽ
7.	są́ñ	ṽñ
8.	są́ñ	ṽñ
9.	sã	ṽ
10.	sã	ṽ

Drill 29 - tones

a snake, low high, ɔwó
he has, low low, ɔwɔ

1.	ɔwó	lh
2.	ɔwɔ	ll
3.	ɔwɔ	ll
4.	ɔwó	lh
5.	ɔwó	lh
6.	ɔwɔ	ll
7,	ɔwó	lh
8.	ɔwɔ	ll
9.	ɔwɔ	ll
10.	ɔwó	lh

Drill 30 - tones

I don't buy, llh, mḛ̃ntó
I wouldn't buy, hlh, mḛ̃ntó

1.	mḛ̃ntó	llh
2.	mḛ̃ntó	llh
3.	mḛ̃ntó	hlh
4.	mḛ̃ntó	llh
5.	mḛ̃ntó	hlh
6.	mḛ̃ntó	hlh
7.	mḛ̃ntó	llh
8.	mḛ̃ntó	hlh
9.	mḛ̃ntó	llh
10.	mḛ̃ntó	llh

Drill 31 - tones

that I may buy, hhh, mḛ̃ntɔ
I wouldn't buy, hlh, mḛ̃ntó

1.	mḛ̃ntɔ	hhh
2.	mḛ̃ntó	hlh
3.	mḛ̃ntɔ	hhh
4.	mḛ̃ntó	hlh
5.	mḛ̃ntó	hlh
6.	mḛ̃ntó	hlh
7.	mḛ̃ntɔ	hhh
8.	mḛ̃ntɔ	hhh
9.	mḛ̃ntó	hlh
10.	mḛ̃ntó	hlh

Drill 32 - tones

that I may buy, hhh, mḛ̃ntɔ
I don't buy, llh, mḛ̃ntó

1.	mḛ̃ntɔ	hhh
2.	mḛ̃ntó	llh
3.	mḛ̃ntó	llh
4.	mḛ̃ntɔ	hhh
5.	mḛ̃ntɔ	hhh
6.	mḛ̃ntó	llh
7.	mḛ̃ntó	llh
8.	mḛ̃ntɔ	hhh
9.	mḛ̃ntó	llh
10.	mḛ̃ntɔ	hhh

Drill 33 - statement and question

that I may buy, statement, mɛ́ntɔ.
Should I buy, question, mɛ́ntɔ?

1.	mɛ́ntɔ?	q
2.	mɛ́ntɔ	s
3.	mɛ́ntɔ	s
4.	mɛ́ntɔ?	q
5.	mɛ́ntɔ	s
6.	mɛ́ntɔ?	q
7.	mɛ́ntɔ	s
8.	mɛ́ntɔ	s
9.	mɛ́ntɔ?	q
10.	mɛ́ntɔ?	q

Drill 34 - tones

a girl, lhhh, abáawa
a servant girl, lllh, abaawá

1.	abaawá	lllh
2.	abaawá	lllh
3.	abáawa	lhhh
4.	abáawa	lhhh
5.	abáawa	lhhh
6.	abaawá	lllh
7.	abáawa	lhhh
8.	abaawá	lllh
9.	abáawa	lhhh
10.	abaawá	lllh

Drill 35 - tones and length

mouse, llh, ạkurá
village, lllh, ạkuraá

1.	ạkurá	llh
2.	ạkuraá	lllh
3.	ạkurá	llh
4.	ạkurá	llh
5.	ạkuraá	lllh
6.	ạkuraá	lllh
7.	ạkurá	llh
8.	ạkuraá	lllh
9.	ạkuraá	lllh
10.	ạkurá	llh

Drill 36 - tones

already, lll, dedạw
an old thing, hll, dédạw

1.	dedạw	lll
2.	dedạw	lll
3.	dedạw	lll
4.	dédạw	hll
5.	dedạw	lll
6.	dédạw	hll
7.	dédạw	hll
8.	dédạw	hll
9.	dedạw	lll
10.	dédạw	hll

Drill 37 - tones

an agreement, llh, mmóm
rather, hlh, mmǒm

1.	mmóm	llh
2.	mmǒm	hlh
3.	mmóm	llh
4.	mmǒm	hlh
5.	mmǒm	hlh
6.	mmóm	llh
7.	mmóm	llh
8.	mmǒm	hlh
9.	mmóm	llh
10.	mmóm	llh

Drill 38 - tones

a bear, high high, sísí
to cheat, low low, sısı

1.	sísí	hh
2.	sísí	hh
3.	sısı	ll
4.	sísí	hh
5.	sısı	ll
6.	sísí	hh
7.	sısı	ll
8.	sısı	ll
9.	sísí	hh
10.	sísí	hh

Drill 39 - nasals

palm oil, velar, ŋg, ŋgɓ
it, alveolar, ɛn, ɛnɓ

1.	ŋgɓ	v
2.	ŋgɓ	v
3.	ɛnɓ	a
4.	ŋgɓ	v
5.	ɛnɓ	a
6.	ɛnɓ	a
7.	ŋgɓ	v
8.	ɛnɓ	a
9.	ŋgɓ	v
10.	ɛnɓ	a

Drill 40 - nasal length

to blow a musical instrument,
  short, hyɛ́ñ
bright, long, hyɛnn

1.	hyɛ́ñ	s
2.	hyɛ́ñ	s
3.	hyɛnn	l
4.	hyɛnn	l
5.	hyɛ́ñ	s
6.	hyɛnn	l
7.	hyɛ́ñ	s
8.	hyɛnn	l
9.	hyɛnn	l
10.	hyɛ́ñ	s

Drill 41 - tones

to dedicate, low low, mǒmǎ
forrid, high high, mőma

1.	mǒmǎ	ll
2.	mǒmǎ	ll
3.	mőmǎ	hh
4.	mőmǎ	hh
5.	mǒmǎ	ll
6.	mőmǎ	hh
7.	mőmǎ	hh
8.	mǒmǎ	ll
9.	mőmǎ	hh
10.	mǒmǎ	ll

Drill 42 - tones

car, high low, káà
ring, low high kaá

1.	kaá	lh
2.	káà	hl
3.	kaá	lh
4.	káà	hl
5.	káà	hl
6.	kaá	lh
7.	kaá	lh
8.	káà	hl
9.	kaá	lh
10.	káà	hl

Drill 43 - nasal and oral
vowels

don't wave, nasal, ññyám
don't grind, oral, ñyám

1.	ññyám	n
2.	ññyám	n
3.	ñyám	o
4.	ññyám	n
5.	ñyám	o
6.	ñyám	o
7.	ññyám	n
8.	ñyám	o
9.	ññyám	n
10.	ñyám	o

Drill 44 - tones

wave, high, ñyám
don't wave, low high, ññyám

1.	ñyám	h
2.	ññyám	lh
3.	ñyám	h
4.	ñyám	h
5.	ññyám	lh
6.	ññyám	lh
7.	ñyám	h
8.	ññyám	lh
9.	ññyám	lh
10.	ñyám	h

Drill 45 - tones

he has gone, 1h, wakɔ́
you have gone, hh, wákɔ

1.	wákɔ	hh
2.	wákɔ	hh
3.	wákɔ	hh
4.	wakɔ́	1h
5.	wakɔ́	1h
6.	wákɔ	hh
7.	wakɔ́	1h
8.	wákɔ	hh
9.	wákɔ	hh
10.	wákɔ	hh

Drill 46 - tones

he didn't come, 11h, wammá
you didn't come, h1h, wámmá

1.	wammá	11h
2.	wámmá	h1h
3.	wammá	11h
4.	wammá	11h
5.	wámmá	h1h
6.	wammá	11h
7.	wámmá	h1h
8.	wámmá	h1h
9.	wammá	11h
10.	wammá	11h

Drill 47 - tones

Accra, 1111, Ŋkɛ̀rã́ñ
black ant, 1hhh, ŋkɛ́rã́ñ

1.	Ŋkɛ̀rã́ñ	1111
2.	ŋkɛ́rã́ñ	1hhh
3.	Ŋkɛ̀rã́ñ	1111
4.	ŋkɛ́rã́ñ	1hhh
5.	ŋkɛ́rã́ñ	1hhh
6.	Ŋkɛ̀rã́ñ	1111
7.	ŋkɛ́rã́ñ	1hhh
8.	ŋkɛ́rã́ñ	1hhh
9.	Ŋkɛ̀rã́ñ	1111
10.	ŋkɛ́rã́ñ	1hhh

Drill 48 - tones

here I am, hhh, mínnɪ
I don't have, 11h, mínní

1.	mínní	11h
2.	mínní	11h
3.	mínnɪ	hhh
4.	mínnɪ	hhh
5.	mínní	11h
6.	mínní	11h
7.	mínnɪ	hhh
8.	mínnɪ	hhh
9.	mínní	11h
10.	mínnɪ	hhh

13

Unit 2

Basic Dialogue

-A-

mã	to give, present; cause let; for, on behalf of
akyế	a becoming clear or visible, a coming-forth
1 °Mã akyế	Good morning. ('/I/ bid /you/ dawning. ')

-B-

yaa	a response to greetings
oñů̌ą́ (ñů̌ą) (pl. ą-nǒm)	brother, sister
2 Yąą ñů̌ą́.	Yes, brother.

-A-

wǫ́, wǫ, w-, wú, wu	your (sg.)
ɛhố	the whole body; exterior; at, by, near
tę	to perceive, feel, hear; live, dwell; speak a language
°sế̃	what, how
3 Wǫ hố tę sế̃?	How are you?

-B-

mẽ, mĩ, m-, mế, mĩ́	my
°yɛ	to be, become; do, make; amount to; seem; be in good condition

14

4   Mɛ̃ hɔ́ yɛ.   I'm fine.

        na   and, but

        ńsǫ   also, too

5   Na wǫ ńsǫ, wǫ hɔ́ tɛ sɛ̃́n?   And you, how are you?

- A -

6   Mɛ̃ hɔ́ yɛ.   I'm fine.

        ofíe (fìe) (pl. e-)   home, house

7   Ofíe tɛ sɛ̃́n?   How is everything at home?

- B -

        °dɛ̧ɛ   to have, possess; be, be in
                                         a state of; continue, keep
                                         on; cause, make

        bokɔɔ   soft, tender, cheap

8   Ofíe dɛ̧ bokɔɔ.   Everything is fine at home.
                                     ('Home is /in a state of/soft.')

Notes

1. /Mã̀ akyɛ́/ is usually //maakye//.

2. /ñũá̧/ means either brother or sister, but it is used in greetings as a matter of politeness. /Ya̧a̧ ñũá̧/ is a customary way of
acknowledging a greeting; it could be just as well translated,
'thank you' or 'good morning'. This response is used by persons of
about the same age and social status.

3. /yaa ñũá̧/ is ya̧a̧ ñũá̧/. See vowel harmony rules below. /u/
followed by /a̧/ is similar to the French semi-vowel 'u', e.g.,
/ñũá̧/.

4.   /sɛ́ñ/ ıs Ashantı Twı. /ɛdéŋ/ or /déŋ/ ıs Akuapım Twı. In 1961 the Bureau of Ghana Languages ıssued <u>Language Guıde</u>'s for the varıous Twı dıalects wıth the recommended spellıngs. Sınce most Twı texts prınted before thıs tıme are based on Akuapım, ıt ıs necessary to know the forms for both dıalects.

5.   /yɛ/ 'to be ın good condıtıon', ıs /yé/ ın Akuapım.

6.   Many words that end ın a sıngle vowel ın Akuapım have a dıphthong ın Ashantı:

	Akuapım	Ashantı
house	ofí	ofíe
thıng	odę́	adéɛ
fufu	fufú	fufúo
caretaker	ɔhwɛ́fɔ̧	ɔhwɛ́fɔ̧ɔ

7.   The noun prefıxes /ɔ, o, ɛ, e/ are usually omıtted ıf they are not wıth the fırst word ın the sentence, e.g., /Yạạ nũą́/. Other noun prefıxes aren't usually omıtted.

8.   It ıs necessary to use /hɛ̃́/ when askıng concernıng one's health or physıcal condıtıon. If /hɛ̃́/ ıs not used, one ıs askıng for a descrıptıon, e.g., /Wǫ yę́rę tę sɛ́ñ/, 'What kınd of wıfe do you have?' ı.e., tall, fat, dark-haıred, etc.

9.   There are two serıes of vowels ın Twı or Akan: a tense or outer serıes, and a lax or ınner serıes.

Tense serıes:	ı	e	ą	o	u
Lax serıes:	ę	ɛ	a	ɔ	ǫ

     The relatıonshıp of the two serıes ıs perhaps more easıly seen ın a vowel trıangle dıagram.

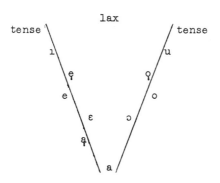

There are limitations as to which vowels can precede or
follow certain other vowels.   These limitations are called vowel
harmony.

Vowel harmony rules.

I.   Lax vowels followed by /ɪ/, /ą/, or /u/ are replaced by
the next highest (see vowel triangle diagram) vowel in the tense
series.

ę	is replaced by	ɪ
ɛ		e
a		ą
ɔ		o
ǫ		u

II.   After /a/, /ɛ/, or /ɔ/, /e/ and /o/ are replaced by the
next highest vowel in the lax series:

e	is replaced by	ę
o		ǫ

III.   Rule I takes precedence over Rule II.

17

IV All contiguous vowels are in the same series. If there
is a tense vowel in a diphthong, all the vowels of the diphthong
will be of the tense series.

10. The vowels of subject and possessive pronouns are determined
by vowel harmony. Notice the underlined vowels:

mẽyɛ	I am	yɛyɛ	we are
wọyè	you (sg.) are	mõyè	you (pl.) are
ọyɛ	he, she, it is	wọyɛ	they are
ɛyɛ	it is	ɛyɛ	they are
mĩhu	I see	yehũ	we see
wũhũ	you (sg.) see	mũhũ	you (pl.) see
ohũ	he, she, it sees	wohũ	they see

The third person singular /ɔ- ∼o-/ often translates 'it'
when referring to animals.

The third person impersonal prefix /ɛ-∼e-/ is always used
for inanimates (including ghosts), but it is occasionally used
when referring to animals in a general way.

mẽ bá	my child	yɛ bá	our child
wọ bá	your (sg.) child	mõ bá	your (pl.) child
nẽ bá	his, her, its child	wón nõ bá	their child
mĩ ñũạ	my brother	yé ñũạ	our brother
wú ñũạ	your (sg.) brother	mú ñũạ	your (pl.) brother
nĩ ñũạ	his, her, its brother	wón nú ñũạ	their brother

In the new orthography, vowel harmony is never indicated in
the possessive pronouns, e.g., /mĩ ñũạ/ is //me nua//. But some
texts printed before the latest spelling revision do have //mi nua//.

/wón nɔ́/ has an alternate form /woŋ/ and is // woŋ//.

/yɛ/ has an alternate form /yɛŋ/. Compare Unit 9 note 15.

The final consonant of /yɛŋ/ and /woŋ/ is homorganic with the following consonant. See notes eleven and twelve of lesson three. Compare Unit 3, notes 11 and 12.

11. The tone pattern of some nouns differs when preceeded by a possessive pronoun from the pattern of the non-possessed form, e.g., /ñũá̧/, 'brother', and /mí ñũá̧/, 'my brother'. If the tones of the possessed form are different, the possessed form is given in parentheses when the word first appears in the lessons, e.g., /okúnu/, 'husband' (kúnu). When the possessed noun has a high tone on the first syllable, the possessive pronoun is low; otherwise, the possessive pronoun is high. See also notes 14 and 15.

12. There are a number of ways of marking the plural of nouns. If the plural form is not the same as the singular, the plural prefix and/or suffix is listed in parentheses with the designation 'pl.' when the word first occurs. The plural of /okúnu/ is /okúnunóm/. It appears as /okúnu/ (kúnu) (pl. -nóm). If the plural is irregular, the entire form is given. If there is more than one plural, the most common plural is given. A hyphen /-/ after a form means the form is a prefix; a hyphen before a form means it is a suffix. Some plurals have both a prefix and a suffix.

New words in the drills.

ɔbá (pl. m-)	child, young one
ɔyɛ́rɛ̧ (pl. -nɔ́m)	wife
papá (pl. -nɔ́m)	father
mãamɛ́ (pl. -nɔ́m)	mother
okúnu (kúnu) (pl. -nɔ́m)	husband

13. Note that /mbá/ is /mmá/. Compare Unit 3 note 12.

14. In part of the exercises in this manual, the student is asked to replace or insert a word or phrase in a previous utterance. The tutor gives a sentence. The student repeats. The tutor gives the word or phrase, which is underlined in the next sentence. The student fits it into the previous utterance.

Example:

Tutor:	Wǫ hő tę sɛ́ñ?
Student:	Wǫ hő tę sɛ́ñ?
Tutor:	Nɛ̃ hő.
Student:	Nɛ̃ hő tę sɛ́ñ?

Lexical Drill A

1.	Wǫ hő tę sɛ́ñ?	How are you?
2.	Nɛ̃ hő tę sɛ́ñ?	How is he?
3.	Mő hő tę sɛ́ñ?	How are you (pl.)?
4.	Wǫn hő tę sɛ́ñ?	How are they?
5.	Wǫ bá hő tę sɛ́ñ?	How is your child?
6.	Wǫ yérę hő tę sɛ́ñ?	How is your wife?
7.	Wǫ́ papá hő tę sɛ́ñ?	How is your father?
8.	Wǫ́ mãamɛ̃́ hő tę sɛ́ñ?	How is your mother?
9.	Wú ñúą hő tę sɛ́ñ?	How is your brother?
10.	Wú̧ kúnu hő tę sɛ́ñ?	How is your husband?

Lexical Drill B

1.	Mẽ hố yɛ.	I am fine.
2.	Nẽ hố yɛ.	He is fine.
3.	Yɛ hố yɛ.	We are fine.
4.	Woŋ hố yɛ.	They are fine.
5.	Mẽ bá hố yɛ.	My child is fine.
6.	Mẽ yɛ́rɛ hố yɛ.	My wife is fine.
7.	Mɛ́ papá hố yɛ.	My father is fine.
8.	Mɛ́ mãamɛ́ hố yɛ.	My mother is fine.
9.	Mí ñúạ hố yɛ.	My brother is fine.
10.	Mí kúnu hố yɛ.	My husband is fine.

Lexical Drill C

1.	Ɔyɛ nɛ́ mãamɛ́.	She is his mother.
2.	Ɔyɛ nɛ́ papá.	He is his father.
3.	Mẽyɛ nɛ́ papá.	I am his father.
4.	Mẽyɛ ní ñúạ.	I am his brother.
5.	Wɔ́yɛ̀ ní ñúạ.	You are her brother.
6.	Wɔ́yɛ̀ nɛ̃ bá.	You are her child.
7.	Ɔyɛ nɔ̃ bá.	She is his child.
8.	Ɔyɛ nɛ́ yɛ́rɛ.	She is his wife.
9.	Ɔyɛ ní kúnu.	He is her husband.
10.	Mẽyɛ ní kúnu.	I am her husband.

Lexical Drill D

1. Yɛyɛ nɛ̃ mmá.   We are his children.

2. Móyɛ̀ nɛ̃ mmá.   You are his children.

3. Móyɛ̀ nɪ́ ñúɐ̧nõ̃m.   You are his brothers and sisters.

4. Wɔyɛ nɪ́ ñúɐ̧nõ̃m.   They are her brothers.

5. Wɔyɛ nɛ̃ yɛ́rɛ̧nõ̃m.   They are his wives.

6. Yɛyɛ nɛ̃ yɛ́rɛ̧nõ̃m.   We are his wives.

7. Yɛyɛ wón nṹ kúnunõ̃m.   We are their husbands.

8. Móyɛ̀ wón nṹ kúnunõ̃m.   You (pl.) are their husbands.

9. Móyɛ̀ yɛ́ papánõ̃m.   You (pl.) are our fathers.

10. Wɔyɛ yɛ́ papánõ̃m.   They are our fathers

Lexical Drill E

1. Wɔyɛ mɪ́ ñúɐ̧nõ̃m.   They are my sisters.

2. Wɔyɛ wú ñúɐ̧nõ̃m.   They are your sisters.

3. Yɛyɛ wú ñúɐ̧nõ̃m.   We are your brothers and sisters.

4. Yɛyɛ wón nṹ ñúɐ̧nõ̃m.   We are their brothers.

5. Yɛyɛ wón nṍ mmá.   We are their children.

6. Móyɛ̀ wón nṍ mmá.   You are their children.

7. Móyɛ̀ nɛ̃ mmá.   You are his children.

8. Móyɛ̀ nɛ̃ yɛ́rɛ̧nõ̃m.   You are his wives.

9. Móyɛ̀ yɛ yɛ́rɛ̧nõ̃m.   You are our wives.

10. Wɔyɛ yɛ yɛ́rɛ̧nõ̃m.   They are our wives.

Lexical Drill F

1.	Woyɛ mɛ̃ mmá.	They are my children.
2.	Woyɛ <u>yɛ mmá</u>.	They are <u>our children</u>.
3.	<u>Mɔ̃yɛ̀</u> yɛ mmá.	<u>You are</u> our children.
4.	<u>Mɔ̃yɛ̀</u> <u>wɔ́n nɔ̃̀ mmá</u>.	You are <u>their children</u>.
5.	<u>Yɛyɛ</u> wɔ́n nɔ̃̀ mmá.	We are <u>their children</u>.
6.	Yɛyɛ <u>mɔ̃ mmá</u>.	We are <u>your (pl.) children</u>.
7.	<u>Woyɛ</u> mɔ̃ mmá.	<u>They are</u> your (pl.) children.
8.	Woyɛ <u>wɔ mmá</u>.	They are <u>your (sg.) children</u>.
9.	<u>Yɛyɛ</u> wɔ mmá.	We are <u>your (sg.)</u> children.
10.	Yɛyɛ <u>nɛ̃ mmá</u>.	We are <u>her children</u>.

14. Nouns with a low nasal prefix in the possessed form have a low-tone pronoun possessor, e.g., /mɛ̃ mmà/, 'my child'.

15. When followed by a low tone, /wɔ́n nɔ̃́/ is sometimes /wɔ́n nɔ̃́/.

Unit 3

Basic Dialogue

-A-

ɛdá (pl. n-)	day
ḍwọ	to cool, be cool
anaḍwọ́	night

1   °Mã aḍwọ́.   Good evening.

-B-

owúrà (wurà)	sir, mister, owner
(pl. ạwúrànóm)	

2   Yạạ owúrà.   Yes sir.

-A-

°Twíì	the Akan or Twi language
°anáa	or, a question marker

3   Wọ́tẹ̀ Twíì anáa?   Do you speak Twi? ('You hear Twi or?')

-B-

°áàn, áàné, éè	yes

4   Áàn, mɛtẹ Twíì.   Yes, I speak Twi.

-A-

Bọrọfọ́	English

5   Wọ́tẹ̀ Bọrọfọ́ anáa?   Do you speak English?

-B-

ᵒdą̄ąbí, dą̀bí   no, never

m-, n-, ñ-, ŋ-   not

6   Dą̄ąbí, mēntę́ Bǫrofǫ́.   No, I don't speak English.

-A-

ká̄   to speak, say, talk

wɔ   to be at; have, own

7   Wǫ́ká̄ Twîì ᵒwo fíe aná̄a?   Do you speak Twi at home?

                                               ('You speak Twi is at home
                                               or?')

-B-

8   Á̄ą̀ñ, mēḱá̄ Twîì wo fíe.   Yes, I speak Twi at home.

Notes

1. /owúrà/ is more polite than /oñúą́/ and is used for an older
man or one in a higher social status. The feminine form is
/ą̀wuraá/, madam, lady, landlady, mistress, miss, and does not
indicate marital state.

2. /aná̄a/ is //ana// or //anaa//.

3. /tę/ means to possess both understanding and speaking ability
in a language. /ká̄/ means to speak in a particular language at a
particular time.

4. /Twîì/ is //Twi//.

5. /Bǫrofǫ́/ means 'the language of the Europeans', but English
will be understood if another language is not specified, e.g.,
/Faransę́ɛ Bǫrofǫ́/, 'French'.

25

6. Pay special attention to the short vowels between a consonant and /r/, as in /Bǫrɔfǫ́/. There are no clusters of a consonant plus /r/. It may be difficult for the student to tell which vowel is present. /ę/ is probably the most difficult vowel to hear between a consonant and /r/, e.g., /kę́rá/, 'soul'. Many of these short vowels, especially /ę/, are not indicated in the orthography.

7. Before /i/ and /u/, /ɔ/ is /o/, e.g., /wɔ fíe/ is /wo fíe/ at <u>conversation</u> speed. In slow speech or if there is a pause between /wɔ/ and /fíe/, /wɔ/ is not replaced by /wo/. Vowel harmony across word boundaries is not indicated in the orthography. Also note the examples of /wɔ/ in lexical drill A.

8. /wɔ/ is a verb and means to be located at a given place. Twi has many constructions of the type: subject plus verb plus object plus verb plus or minus object, e.g., /Wǫ́kã̀ Twíî̀ wo fíe anáa?/.

9. /kúro/ is // kurow//.

10. /mú̀/ is very often /m̀/, e.g., /kúro mú̀/ is very often /kúrom̀/ and is // kurow mu// or // kurow m'//.

11. A negative verb is formed by prefixing a <u>low-toned</u> nasal to the verb stem plus a high tone on the last syllable. The nasal is homorganic with the following consonant of the verb stem, i.e., it is made or articulated in the same position as the following consonant:

m	before	m, p, b, f
n		n, w, t, d, s
ŋ		ŋ, k, g, h
ñ		ñ, y, w̌, ky, tw, gy, dw, hy, hw

(Some verbs with secondary tones have a high-toned negative prefix. See Unit 18, note 5.)

12.   Combinations of nasal plus homorganic voiced stop do not
occur. This combination is replaced by a long or geminate
(double) nasal:

	is replaced by	
mb	is replaced by	mm
nd		nn
ñgy		ññ, i.e., /ññy or ñỹ/
ŋg		ṇṇ, i.e., /ŋg/

See also note 17.

13.   Vowel harmony doesn't usually operate across a nasal plus
another consonant: /mɛ̃hṹ/ is replaced by /mĩhṹ/, but /mɛ̃nhṹ/ is
usually not replaced by /mĩnhṹ/. Vowel harmony does operate
across two nasal consonants nearly always.

Substitution Drill A

1.	Mɛ̃tɛ Twíì.	I speak Twi.
2.	Yotɔ Twíì.	We speak Twi.
3.	Ɔtɛ Twíì.	He speaks Twi.
4.	Wotɛ Twíì.	They speak Twi.
5.	Mí kunú tɛ Twíì.	My husband speaks Twi.
6.	Mɛ̃ yérɛ tɛ Twíì.	My wife speaks Twi.
7.	Mɛ̃ mãamɛ̃ tɛ Twíì.	My mother speaks Twi.
8.	Mɛ̃ papá tɛ Twíì.	My father speaks Twi.
9.	Mɛ̃ bá tɛ Twíì.	My child speaks Twi.
10.	Mí ñũa tɛ Twíì.	My brother speaks Twi.

Substitution Drill B

1.	Mḕntę́ Twîì.	I don't speak Twi.	
2.	Yɛntę́ Twîì.	We don't speak Twi.	
3.	Ɔntę́ Twîì.	He doesn't speak Twi.	
4.	Wɔntę́ Twîì.	They don't speak Twi.	
5.	Mí kúnu ntę́ Twîì.	My husband doesn't speak Twi.	
6.	Mɛ̃ yę́rę ntę́ Twîì.	My wife doesn't speak Twi.	
7.	Mɛ́ mãamɛ́ ntę́ Twîì.	My mother doesn't speak Twi.	
8.	Mɛ́ papá ntę́ Twîì.	My father doesn't speak Twi.	
9.	Mɛ̃ bá ntę́ Twîì.	My child doesn't speak Twi.	
10.	Mí ńúą ntę́ Twîì.	My brother doesn't speak Twi.	

Question and Answer Drill A

The tutor gives the question. The student gives the affirmative response.

1.	Wɔ́tę̀ Twîì anáa?	Ã́ą̃ñ, mḕtę Twîì.
2.	Mɔ́tę̀ Twîì anáa?	Ã́ą̃ñ, yɛtę Twîì.
3.	Ɔtę̀ Twîì anáa?	Ã́ą̃ñ, otę Twîì.
4.	Wɔtę̀ Twîì anáa?	Ã́ą̃ñ, wotę Twîì.
5.	Wú kúnu tę Twîì anáa?	Ã́ą̃ñ, mí kúnu tę Twîì.
6.	Wɔ yę́re tę Twîì anáa?	Ã́ą̃ñ, mɛ̃ yę́rę tę Twîì.
7.	Wɔ́ mãamɛ́ tę Twîì anáa?	Ã́ą̃ñ, mɛ́ mãamɛ́ tę Twîì.
8.	Wɔ́ papá tę Twîì anáa?	Ã́ą̃ñ, mɛ́ papá tę Twîì.
9.	Wɔ bá tę Twîì anáa?	Ã́ą̃ñ, mɛ̃ bá tę Twîì.
10.	Wú ńúą tę Twîì anáa?	Ã́ą̃ñ, mí ńúą tę Twîì.

Question and Answer Drill B

Student gives negative answer.

1.	Wǫ́tę̀ Twíì anáa?	Dą̀ą̀bí, mɛ̃ntę́ Twíì.
2.	Mǒtę̀ Twíì anáa?	Dą̀ą̀bí, yɛntę́ Twíì.
3.	Ɔtę Twíì anáa?	Dą̀ą̀bí, ontę́ Twíì.
4.	Wotę Twíì anáa?	Dą̀ą̀bí, wontę́ Twíì.
5.	Wú kùnu tę Twíì anáa?	Dą̀ą̀bí, mí kùnu ntę́ Twíì.
6.	Wǫ yę́re tę Twíì anáa?	Dą̀ą̀bí, mɛ̃ yę́rę ntę́ Twíì.
7.	Wǫ́ mãamɛ́ tę Twíì anáa?	Dą̀ą̀bí, mɛ̃ mãamɛ́ ntę́ Twíì.
8.	Wǫ́ papá tę Twíì anáa?	Dą̀ą̀bí, mɛ̃ papá ntę́ Twíì.
9.	Wǫ bá tę Twíì anáa?	Dą̀ą̀bí, mɛ̃ bá ntę́ Twíì.
10.	Wú ñùą̀ tę Twíì anáa?	Dą̀ą̀bí, mí ñùą̀ ntę́ Twíì.

Lexical Drill A

1.	Mɛ̃wo fíe.	I am at home.
2.	Mɛ̃wo fíe nɔ̃́ mǔ.	I am in the house.
3.	Mɛ̃wo Nkęrã́ñ.	I am at Accra.
4.	Mɛ̃wo fíe bí.	I own a house.
5.	Mɛ̃wo ñùą́.	I have a brother.
6.	Mɛ̃wo Kumásę.	I am at Kumasi.
7.	Mɛ̃wo bá.	I have a child.
8.	Mɛ̃wo pɛ́nsę̀rę.	I have a pencil.
9.	Mɛ̃wo sukúù nɔ̃́ mǔ.	I am in the school.
10.	Mɛ̃wo fíe wo Kumásę.	I have a house in Kumasi.

14. /Ŋkɛráñ/ ıs // Nkran//.

15.   bí   a, an, any, some

     Avoıd the use of /bí/, especıally ın reference to persons, unless you ıntend to mean 'some kınd or other', 'any kınd of', or 'just any kınd'. In lexıcal drıll A sentence four, /bí/ ıs requıred to dıstınguısh 'I own a house' from 'I am at home'. A noun wıthout the followıng demonstratıve or artıcle /nɔ́/, 'the', 'that', ıs ındefınıte, ı.e., ıt translates 'a' or 'an'.

    Grammatıcal Drıll A

    Gıve the negatıve form of the followıng verbs.

	Affırmatıve		Negatıve
1.	tɛ̨	(to feel)	ntɛ̨́
2.	tɛ̨	(to speak)	ntɛ̨́
3.	wɔ	(to have)	nní
4.	dı	(to eat)	nní
5.	yɛ	(to be)	ɛñỹɛ́
6.	yɛ	(to be good)	ɛñỹɛ́
7.	da	(to sleep)	nná
8.	mã	(to gıve)	mmã́
9.	kã́	(to speak)	ŋkã́
10.	sũɛ̨́	(to learn)	nsũɛ̨́
11.	kasa	(to talk)	ŋkasá
12.	da asɛ̨	(to lıe down)	ɛnná asɛ̨
13.	wɔ	(to be at)	nní
14.	hũ	(to see)	nhṹ
15.	twɛ̨	(to cut)	ñtwɛ̨́

16.	tɔ	(to buy)		ntɔ́
17.	kɔ	(to go)		ŋkɔ́
18.	bɛrá	(to come)		mmá
19.	hyɛ	(to insert)		ñhyɛ́
20.	bɔ	(to strike)		mmɔ́

16.   /dąąbí/ is Akuapım and also eastern Ashantı. /dąbí/ is the
form most used in Ashantı and is //dabı/in the new orthography.

17.   The underlying aim of the new (1961) orthography is to pro-
vide a common writing system for all Twı dialects. Since it is
necessary for the system to be readily intelligible to readers of
all dialects, a number of words have been spelled without the
assimilative changes that have taken place in Ashantı dialect.
Noun plurals of stems beginning with voiced stops are not spelled
with geminate nasals, e.g., /nná/, 'days', is //nda//; but the same
assimilation is written in the verbs, e.g., /nná/, 'Don't lie',
'Don't sleep', is //nna//

18.   /ą̃ą̃ñ́/ is //aane// in the new orthography.

31

Unit 4

Basic Dialogue

-A-

| | na | | and, emphatic particle |
| 1 | Sɛ̃n na yɛká thank you wo Twíì mû? | | How do you say 'thank you' in in Twi? |

-B-

	da		to lie, sleep, rest
	asɛ; asɛ́ɛ̀		the lower part; down, under; meaning, sense
2	Mɛ̃da asɛ.		Thanks. ('I lie down.'), ('I prostrate /myself before you/.')
3	Wɔ́tɛ̀ asɛ́ɛ̀ anãa?		Do you understand?

-A-

4	Ãɛ̀ñ, mɛ̃tɛ °wasɛ.		Yes, I understand you.
	ebío		again
5	Ká bío.		Say it again.
	kasa		to talk, speak
	°bɛrɛɛoo		slow, soft, mild
6	Kasa bɛrɛɛoo.		Talk slowly. Talk softly.

-B-

| 7 | Mɛ̃da wasɛ. | | Thank you. |

32

-A-

8   Sɛ́ñ na yɛká̋ <u>you are welcome</u>   How do you say 'you are welcome'

    wo Twíì mú?   in Twi?

-B-

9   °Mmɛ́ ɛnná asę̀.   You are welcome. Don't mention

                                           it. ('Don't cause /yourself/

                                           don't lie down. ')

Notes

1. The first person plural of the Twi verb often translates with
an English passive or impersonal you. /yɛká̋/, literally 'we say',
often corresponds to 'it is said' or 'you say'.

2. /na/, 'and', 'but', joins sentences; /nɛ̋/, 'and', 'with',
connects words. /na/ is put after a word or at the beginning of
a sentence to add emphasis. It often isn't translated into
English. Compare Unit 10, note 10.

3. /wǫ́ asę́ɛ̀/ is usually /wásę̀ɛ̀/ and is // wo ase// or // wo aseɛ//.
If there is an expressed object, i.e., if the sentence tells who
is understood, the student should use /asę/ because /asę́ɛ̀/
doesn't occur often with an object. If there is no expressed
object, use /asę́ɛ̀/ because /asę́/ may be misunderstood. /Wǫ́tę̀
asę?/ may not only mean 'Do you understand?', but also 'Are you
sitting down?', and 'Are you still living?'. /Wǫ́tę̀ asę́ɛ̀?/ means
only 'Do you understand?'.

4. On the telephone <u>only</u> can you say /Mǎtę́ asę/ or /Mǎtę́ asę́ɛ̀/,
with a high tone on /tę́/, meaning 'I understand the meaning or
message'.

33

5. /a/ followed by /y/ is high and front like a French 'a'.
/ɔ/ followed by /ɪ/ is /o/, e.g., /wɔ Twíì/ is /wo Twíì/.
At less than conversation speed or if there is a pause between words, these vowel replacements don't occur. Vowel harmony
across word boundaries is never shown in the orthography.

6. /ebío/ has an alternate form /ebɪbío/. /ebío/ is the more
common form.

7. /Kasa bɛrɛɛoo/ means <u>both</u> 'Talk slowly and softly.' and is
//brɛɛ oo// or //brɛɛw//. /oo/ is an emphasis marker.

8. The imperative (command form) singular is the same as the
habitual stem, but with all low tones, e.g., /kasa/, 'talk',
addressing one person. The imperative plural prefixes /mõn-/,
e.g., /Mõŋkasa/, 'talk', with all high tones.

9. Before initial /-nn/, /ɛ-/ occurs, e.g., /nná asę̧/ is /ɛnná
asę̧/.

When a word beginning with a vowel is preceeded by a word
ending in a vowel, the final vowel of the preceeding word is
usually replaced by the same vowel as that which begins the
following word, i.e., a long or rearticulated vowel occurs, e.g.,
/Mmá ɛnná asę̧/ is /Mmɛ́ ɛnná asę̧/, but it is // Mma ɛnnaase//.

10. Notice the <u>two</u> negatives in /M̲m̲ɛ́ ɛ̲n̲ná asę̧./.

Lexical Drill A

1. Wǫ́tę̧ asę́ę́ anáa?	Do you understand?
2. Wǫ́tę̧ °<u>masę̧</u> anáa?	Do you understand me?
3. Wǫ́tę́ °<u>nasę̧</u> anáa?	Do you understand him?
4. Wǫ́tę̧ <u>wɔn asę̧</u> anáa?	Do you understand them?
5. Wǫ́tę́ <u>yɛn asę̧</u> anáa?	Do you understand us?

Lexical Drill B

1. Ɔtɛ asɛ́ɛ̀ anáa?   Does he understand?

2. Ɔtɛ <u>masɛ</u> anáa?   Does he understand me?

3. Ɔtɛ ^o<u>wasɛ</u> anáa?   Does he understand you?

4. Ɔtɛ ^o<u>másɛ̀</u> anáa?   Does he understand you (pl.)?

5. Ɔtɛ <u>wɔn asɛ</u> anáa?   Does he understand them?

Lexical Drill C

1. Mɛ̃tɛ asɛ́ɛ̀.   I understand.

2. Mɛ̃tɛ <u>wásɛ̀</u>.   I understand you.

3. Mɛ̃tɛ <u>nasɛ</u>.   I understand him.

4. Mɛ̃tɛ <u>wɔn asɛ</u>.   I understand them.

5. Mɛ̃tɛ <u>másɛ̀</u>.   I understand you (pl.).

Lexical Drill D

1. Ɔtɛ asɛ́ɛ̀.   He understands.

2. Ɔtɛ <u>masɛ</u>.   He understands me.

3. Ɔtɛ <u>wasɛ</u>.   He understands you.

4. Ɔtɛ <u>másɛ̀</u>.   He understands you (pl.).

5. Ɔtɛ <u>wɔn asɛ</u>.   He understands them.

Lexical Drill E

1. Nɛ̃́ mãamɛ̃́ ntɛ̃́ Bɔrɔfɔ́.   His mother doesn't know English.

2. Nɛ̃́ mãamɛ̃́ <u>tɛ Twíì</u>.   His mother <u>knows Twi</u>.

3. <u>Ɔnɛ̃́ nɛ̃́ mãamɛ̃́</u> tɛ Twíì.   <u>He and his mother</u> know Twi.

4. Ɔnɛ̃́ nɛ̃́ mãamɛ̃́ <u>kã́ Twíì</u>.   He <u>speaks Twi</u> with his mother.

5. <u>Mɛ̃ nɛ̃́ mɛ̃́ papá</u> kã́ Twíì.   I speak Twi with my father.

6. Mɛ̃ nɛ̃ mɛ̃ papá tɛ̞   My father and I know Gã.
   Ŋkɛ̞rã̃ñ

7. Mí ñûą̞ tɛ̞ Ŋkɛ̞rã̃ñ.   My sister knows Gã.

8. Mí ñûą̞ tɛ̞ Ŋkɛ̞rã̃ñ.   My sister lives at Accra.

9. Mɛ̃ bá tɛ̞ Ŋkɛ̞rã̃ñ.   My child lives in Accra.

10. Mɛ̃ bá wɔ Ŋkɛ̞rã̃ñ.   My child is at Accra.

Lexical Drill F

1. Wɔká Twíì wo sukúù.   They speak Twi at school.

2. Yesûą̞ Twíì wo sukúù.   They study Twi at school.

3. Yesuą̞́ Twíì wɔ Ŋkɛ̞rã̃ñ. We study Twi at Accra.

4. Wɔ̞̀wò fíe wɔ Ŋkɛ̞rã̃ñ.   You have a house at Accra.

5. Wɔ̞̀wò fíe wɔ Tamalɛ̞.   You have a house at Tamale.

6. Mɔ̃́ papá wɔ Tamalɛ̞.   Your father is at Tamale.

7. Mɔ̃́ papá wo fíe.   Your father is at home.

8. Yɛ yɛ̞́rɛ̞nõm wo fíe.   Our wives are at home.

9. Yɛ yɛ̞́rɛ̞nõm nní fíe.   Our wives aren't at home.

10. Mí kùnu nní fíe.   My husband isn't at home.

Lexical Drill G

1. Kasa bɛ̞rɛɛoo.   Talk slow.

2. Kasa dɛ̃ñ.   Talk loud.

3. Ɛyɛ́ dɛ̃ñ.   It is hard.

4. Ɛyɛ́ bɛtɛɛ.   It is soft.

5. Mɛ̃ nsá yɛ bɛtɛɛ.   My hand is tender.

6. Mẽ nsá yɛ <u>téntẽn</u>.	My arm is <u>long</u>.
7. Mẽ <u>káà nő</u> yɛ tẽntẽn.	<u>My car</u> is long.
8. Mẽ káà nő <u>ñỹέ</u>.	My car is <u>no good</u>.
9. Nẽ <u>pénsèrɛ nő</u> ñỹέ.	His pencil is bad.
10. Nẽ pénsèrɛ nő <u>da hó</u>.	His pencil <u>is lying there</u>.

New words in the drills.

| pénsèrɛ (pénsèrɛ) | pencil |
| káà (káà) | automobile |

Lexical Drill H

1. Mẽtɛ Twíì.	I speak Twi.
2. Mẽtɛ <u>Nkɛráñ</u>.	I speak <u>Gã</u>.
3. Mẽtɛ <u>Nkɛráñ</u>.	<u>I live at</u> Accra.
4. Mẽtɛ <u>asɛ́ɛ̀</u>.	I <u>understand</u>.
5. Mẽtɛ <u>asɛ</u>.	I'm <u>sitting down</u>.
6. Mẽtɛ <u>dóŋ nő</u>.	I hear <u>the bell</u>.
7. Mẽtɛ <u>mẽ mãamẽ́ ásὲm</u>.	I <u>obey my mother</u>.
8. Mẽtɛ <u>akőññúá só</u>.	I'm sitting <u>in a chair</u>.
9. Mẽtɛ <u>sɛ́ɛ̀ wo</u>.	I am <u>as you are</u>.
10. Mẽtɛ <u>sɛ́ɛ̀ abofára</u>.	I am <u>like a child</u>.

New words in drills.

ɛdóŋ, ɔdóŋ (pl. n-)	bell
akőññúá (pl. ŋ-)	chair, stool
asɛ́m (ásὲm) (pl. n-)	word, saying, story, talk
tɛ ... asɛ́m	to obey

37

sɛ́ɛ̀
: as, like, that (as in 'I said <u>that</u> ... '

tɛ̨ sɛ́ɛ̀
: to be the same as, be in the same condition or position as

°abɔfára (pl. m-)
: child

ɛsɔ́, sɔ́
: top, upper part; on, up, upon, over, above

11. /masɛ̨/ is // me ase// or // m' ase//.
/nasɛ̨/ is // ne ase// or // n' ase//.
/másɛ̨̀/ is // mo ase// or // m' ase//.
/wásɛ̨̀/ is // wo ase// or // w' ase//.
Usually elision is not indicated in the orthography.

12. /nɛ́/ means 'and' or 'with'. /ɔnɛ́/ is a contraction of
/ɔnɔ́ nɛ́/. /ɔnɛ́ nɛ́ mãamɛ́/ is a contraction of /ɔnɔ́ nɛ́ nɛ́ mãamɛ́/.

13. /sũą́/ means 'to study', 'learn', 'imitate', 'follow the
example of'.

14. /Ŋkɛ̨rãñ/ or Gã is also the name of the language of the
/Ŋkɛ̨rãñ/ or Gã people. The Gã live in the region of Accra. Twi
and Gã are both Kwa languages, i.e., they are related to each
other and "descended" from the same earlier form of the language,
as French and Spanish are both Romance languages "descended"
from Latin.

15. /wɔ/ has a suppletive negative, i.e., a different word is
used to form the negative. /nní/ is the negative of /wɔ/. /nní/
is the negative of /di/, 'to use, eat, contain, last, exist'.

16. /abǫfára/ is // abɔfra//. /abǫfára/ is used only of humans.
/ɔbá/ may be used for the young of animals and also as a
diminutive.

17. Phrases like /Twîì mú/, 'in Twi' are possessive nominal
compounds. Literally, this compound is 'Twi's insides'. This
compound noun is the object of the verb /wɔ/. Modifiers of
various kinds may occur between the possessive and possessed
nouns. Seé Unit 6, note 22.

Unit 5

Basic Dialogue

-A-

ahá	weariness
1 Mã ahá.	Good afternoon.

-B-

2 Yɛɛ owúrà.	Yes sir.

-A-

ɛhɔ́ (pl. ɛ-nɔ̃m)	there; that; from
3 Owúrà Owúsú wɔ hó anáa?	Is Mr. Owusu in?

-B-

ɔ-, onɔ́	he, she, it
ɛhá (pl. ɛ-nɔ̃m)	here; this
4 Áàñ, ɔwo há.	Yes, he is here.

-A-

tumí	to be able, can, to be well-versed in, to have permission
hũ, hũnṹ	to see
onɔ́, nɔ́	him, her, it
5 Mɪtumí ɦ̣ũ nɔ́ anáa?	Can I see him?

-B-

yɛ	we
ᵒfɛrɛ́	to call

6 ᵒYɛfᶓrɛ̀w̄ sɛ́ñ?   What's your name?

                                    ('We call you what?')

                        -A-

7 Yɛfᶓrɛ́ mē Kofí Asantᶒ.   My name is Kofi Asante.

                        -B-

        kā̀   to speak, tell, say

        kyᶓrɛ́   to show, teach, advise

        sɛ́ɛ̀   that

8 Mɛ́kā̀ kyᶓrɛ́ nō̌ sɛ́ɛ̀ wᶗ̀wò há.   I will tell him you are here.

                        Notes

1. /ɔwɔ hɔ́/ usually means 'He, she, or it is there'; but if you
come into or upto a building and ask /ɔwɔ hɔ́?/, you are asking,
'Is he in?', 'Is he in the building?', or 'Is he around here
somewhere'. The affirmative response will probably be /ɔwɔ há/,
'He is here'. However, if the person answering doesn't know
just where the other person is, he may answer you /ɔwɔ hɔ́/,
'He is around here somewhere'.

2. /ɔwɔ há/ usually means 'He, she, or it is here'; but if you
come into or upto a building and ask /ɔwɔ há?/, you are asking,
'Is this his place?', i.e., 'Does he live here?', or 'Does he
work here?'. The affirmative answer is /ɔwɔ há/, 'This is his
place'. You may then ask /ɔwɔ hɔ́?/.

3. After a noun /há/ and /hɔ́/ can be translated like demonstra-
tives, e.g., /ofie há/, 'this house', and /ofie hɔ́/, 'that
house'.

4. After /tumí/ the following verb is in the consecutive form,
which has an /á- ~ą́-/ prefix. The consecutive form often
corresponds to an English complimentary infinitive, e.g.,

                        41

/Mĭtumí ákɔ̀/, 'I am able to go'. The implication of this form is often 'I am equal to /the task/', or '/I am sure/ I can do it /because I have done it before/'. It may also be used to ask and give permission, as in this dialogue.

The student should avoid the use of /tumí/ in the future (See note 9), when addressing someone because this form has a pejorative implication that you don't think the other person can do something or that you are daring the other person to do something, e.g., /Wóbetùmi yέ sέñ?/. '/Just/ what could you /possibly/ do?' implying that the person addressed is not equal to the situation being discussed. If following a verb not ending in high tone, the consecutive prefix is low. Subject pronouns are not prefixed to the consecutive after /tumí/ except in the first singular, and this is not common. See also Unit 10, note 8.

The first person future of /tumí/ implies that you think you can do something but you aren't certain because you really don't know or you've never done the particular thing before, e.g., /Métùmi ákɔ̀/, 'I will be able to go', or '/I think maybe/ I can go'. The student ahould avoid use of /tumí/ in the future when talking of himself because he will be thought to be boasting.

5.   /sέέ/, 'that', is required to introduce subordinate clause after verbs of 'saying' or 'telling'. See also Unit 18, note 5.

6.   Many speakers use /hũ̌/ before an object pronoun and /hũnũ̌/ elsewhere. Some use these forms interchangeably. Some use /hũ̌/ before an object and /hũnũ̌/ without an object.

7.   /fɛ̞rέ/ is //frɛ/. /Yɛfɛ̞rέw/ is a contraction and alternate form of /Yɛfɛ̞rέ wɔ̞/ and is //Yɛfrɛ w'// or //Yɛfrɛ wɔ//

8.   The use of the first person plural, i.e., the we-form, often corresponds to English passive. /Yɛfɛ̞rέ nɔ̃ sέñ?/, 'What is it called?', but literally 'We call it what?'.

The student will also hear /Wu dĭñ dę̌ dέñ?/. /edĭñ/ means 'name', 'reputation', and 'fame'. This is an Akuapim construction.

9. The positive future is marked by the prefix /bé-/, e.g., /wóbɛko/, 'you will go.' In the first person singular, a contracted form occurs, e.g., /méko/, 'I will go'. Verbs stems that are low high or low low in the present are mid high in the future. High low stems are high high in the future. Other stems have the same tones in the future as in the present.

10. You can /kấ/ a story or something. /kấ kyɛrɛ́/ has the meaning 'to convey information' or 'relate'.

11. Order of verb objects is the same as English; the indirect object (1) preceeds the direct (2) e.g., /Mékấ kyɛrɛ́ nố (1) sɛ́ɛ́ wówò hấ (2)/, 'I will tell him (1) you are here (2)'.

Pattern Drill A

1.	Yefɛrɛ́w sɛ́ɲ?	What's your name?
2.	Yefɛrɛ́ nố sɛ́ɲ?	What's his name?
3.	Yefɛrɛ́ mố sɛ́ɲ?	What are your names?
4.	Yefɛrɛ́ won sɛ́ɲ?	What are their names?
5.	Yefɛrɛ́ wó kunu sɛ́ɲ?	What's your husband's name?
6.	Yefɛrɛ́ wo yɛ́rɛ sɛ́ɲ?	What's your wife's name?
7.	Yefɛrɛ́ wó mấamɛ̃́ sɛ́ɲ?	What's your mother's name?
8.	Yefɛrɛ́ wó papá sɛ́ɲ?	What's your father's name?
9.	°Yefɛrɛ́ wo bá sɛ́ɲ?	What's your child's name?
10.	°Yefɛrɛ́ wó ɲua sɛ́ɲ?	What's your brother's name?

Lexical Drill A

1.	Yefɛrɛ́ mɛ̃ Kofí.	My name is Kofi.
2.	Yefɛrɛ́ nố Kofí.	His name is Kofi.
3.	Yefɛrɛ́ yen Kofí nɛ́ Afúá.	Our names are Kofi and Afua.
4.	Yefɛrɛ́ won Kofí nɛ́ Afúá.	Their names are Kofi and Afua.

43

5.   Yɛfɛrɛ mí kunu Kofí.   <u>My husband's</u> name is <u>Kofi</u>.

6.   Yɛfɛrɛ mɛ̃ yɛrɛ Afúá.   <u>My wife's</u> name is <u>Afua</u>.

7.   Yɛfɛrɛ mɛ̃ mãamɛ̃ Afúá.   <u>My mother's</u> name is <u>Afua</u>.

8.   Yɛfɛrɛ mɛ̃ papá Kofí.   <u>My father's</u> name is <u>Kofi</u>.

9.   Yɛfɛrɛ mɛ̃ bá Kofí.   <u>My child's</u> name is <u>Kofi</u>.

10. Yɛfɛrɛ mí ñúá Kofí.   <u>My brother's</u> name is <u>Kofi</u>.

Pattern Drill B

Answer affirmatively.

1.   Ɔwo hó?   Is he there?

     Áàñ, ɔwɔ hó.   Yes, he is there.

2.   Ɔwɔ há?   Is he here?

     Áàñ, ɔwɔ há.   Yes, he is here.

3.   Ɔwo fíe?   Is he at home?

     Áàñ, ɔwɔ fíe.   Yes, he is at home.

4.   Ɔwo fíe nó mũ?   Is he in the house?

     Áàñ, ɔwɔ fíe nó mṹ.   Yes, he is in the house.

5.   Ɔwo fíe há?   Is he in this house?

     Áàñ, ɔwɔ fíe há.   Yes, he is in this house.

6.   Ɔwo fíe hó?   Is he in that house?

     Áàñ, ɔwɔ fíe hó.   Yes, he is in that house.

Pattern Drill C

Answer negatively.

1. Owɔ hó?   Is he in?

   Dąąbí, ɔnní hó.   No, he is not around.

2. Owɔ há?   Is this his place?

   Dąąbí, ɔnní há.   No, this isn't his place.

3. Owo fíe?   Is he at home?

   Dąąbí, ɔnní fíe.   No, he isn't at home.

4. Owo fíe nó mú?   Is he in the house?

   Dąąbí, ɔnní fíe nó mú.   No, he isn't in the house.

5. Owo fíe há?   Does he own this house?

   Dąąbí, ɔnní fíe há.   No, he doesn't own this house.

6. Owo fíe hó?   Does he own that house?

   Dąąbí, ɔnní fíe hó.   No, he doesn't own that house.

Pattern Drill D

1. Mɛ́kɔ hó.   I will go there.

2. Wǫ́bɛkɔ hó.   You will go there.

3. Wǫ́bɛkɔ nné.   You will go today.

4. Ɔbɛ́kɔ nné.   He will go today.

5. Ɔbɛ́kɔ okyénã́.   He will go tomorrow.

6. Yɛbɛ́kɔ okyénã́.   We will go tomorrow.

7. Yɛbɛ́kɔ bío.   We will go again.

8. Wǫ́bɛkɔ bío.   You will go again.

9. Wǫbɛkɔ <u>Tamalɛ</u>.   You will go to <u>Tamale</u>.

10. Wɔbɛ́kɔ Tamalɛ.   <u>They will go</u> to Tamale.

11. Wɔbɛ́kɔ <u>Kumásɛ</u>.   They will go to <u>Kumasi</u>.

12. Mɛ́kɔ Kumásɛ.   <u>I will go</u> to Kumasi.

Pattern Drill E

1. Mɛ́ba hó.   I will be there.

2. Mɛ́ba <u>dáñ mú</u>.   I will come <u>into the house</u>.

3. Mɛ́tùmì ǫ̀hũ̀ nɔ wɔ dáñ mú. I can see him in the room
                        privately.

4. Mɛ́tùmì ǫ̀hũ̀ nɔ̃ <u>wo sukúù</u>. I can see him <u>at school</u>.

5. <u>Mɛ̃̀ nɛ̃̀ nɔ̃ bɛ́kàsa</u> wo sukúù. <u>I will talk to him</u> at school.

6. Mɛ̃̀ nɛ̃̀ nɔ̃ bɛ́kàsa <u>wo fíe</u>. I will talk to him <u>at home</u>.

7. <u>Mɛ́kã́ kyɛ̀rɛ́ nɔ̃ sɛ́ɛ̀ wǫ̀wò</u>   I will tell him <u>you</u> are at
    fíe.   home.

8. Mɛ́ka kyɛ̀rɛ́ nɔ̃ sɛ́ɛ̀ <u>wǫ̀bɛba</u> I will tell him you <u>will be</u>
    há.   <u>here</u>.

9. <u>Mɛ̃̀ yɛ́rɛ</u> bɛ́ba há.   <u>My wife</u> will come here.

10. Mɛ̃̀ yɛ́re <u>bɛ́fɛ̀rɛ wǫ</u>.   My wife <u>will call you</u>.

Pattern Drill F

1. Yɛfɛ̀rɛ́ nɔ̃ sɛ̃́ñ?   What is his name?

2. Yɛfɛ̀rɛ́ nɔ̃ <u>Kofí</u>.   His name is <u>Kofi</u>.

3. <u>Mɛ́kã́ kyɛ̀rɛ́</u> Kofí.   <u>I will tell</u> Kofi.

4. Mɛ́kã́ kyɛ̀rɛ́ <u>woŋ</u>.   I will tell <u>them</u>.

5. <u>Otumí fɛ̀rɛ́</u> woŋ.   <u>He can phone</u> them.

6. Otumí fɛ̀rɛ́ <u>mɛ̃̀</u>.   He can call <u>me</u>.

7. Ɔbéká kyęré mɛ̃.   He will tell me.
8. Ɔbéká kyęré wo.   He will tell you.
9. Ɔntę wo̧.   He doesn't hear you.
10. Ɔntę́ wasę.   He doesn't understand you.

New words in the drills

    ɔdán (pl. a-)   building, house, room, apartment

12. In addition to syllable tone, Twi also has sentence tone or intonation, i.e., tone used to distinguish statements and questions; compare English 'John is here.', and 'John is here?' In Twi the end of a sentence is signalled by a depression of the entire tone register on the last syllable, i.e., no matter what the phonemic status of the tone is, it will be lower on the absolute scale than a non-final tone of the same phoneme. And also the voice trails off to silence. In addition, a question signalled by intonation (i.e., not by a question word), the register of the whole sentence is elevated, and the last syllable falls down to the same level as the end of a statement. This of course means that there is a longer fall on the last syllable of a question than of a statement because the fall of the question begins higher. For this reason, it would probably be helpful to use an inverted question mark /¿/ at the beginning of a question marked by intonation.

    Twi orthography like English uses at the end of a sentence a period /./ to mark statement intonation and a question mark /?/ to mark question intonation. When there is a question word, e.g., /sɛ́n/, statement intonation is used; however, a question mark is still written. This manual follows the orthography in this usage.

13. Stative verbs such as /wo/, 'to be at', aren't usually inflected for tense. /ba/, 'to come', is used as a suppletive future for /wo/. /méba há/, 'I will come here', also is used like English, 'I will be here'. Compare Unit 10, note 10.

Unit 6

Basic Dialogue

-A-

1	Agoo	Is anybody there?

-B-

2	Amẽe	Come in.

-A-

	ɛpó (pl. m-)	joint, bump, knob
	°ɛɛ	a question marker
3	Wọ mpó mũ ɛɛ?	How are you?
		('Your joints' in, what about?')

-B-

4	Mẽ mpó mũ dẹɛ bokɔɔ.	I'm fine.

-A-

	ɛdẹɛ̃ñ	what, what thing
	yɛ́	to make, do
5	Ɛdẹɛ̃n na °wóọyɛ?	What are you making?

-B-

	nóá	to boil, cook by boiling
	fufúo	fufu
6	°Mẽenóá fufúo.	I'm making fufu.
	pɛ	to like, be fond of, want,
		seek, provide, try to get

7	Wóọpɛ̀ fufúo anáa?	Do you like fufu?

-A-

pá   good, much

pápaapa, pápapapa   very good, very much

8 Mɛ̃pɛ fufúo pápaapa.   I like fufu very much.

-B-

ampesíe   ampesı

sɛ̃ɲ   to surpass, pass; more
                                than, than

9 Mɛ̃pɛ ampesíe sɛ̃ɲ fufúo.   I like ampesı better than fufu.

                                ('I like ampesı exceed fufu.')

Notes

1. /agʋʋ/ is a verbal signal to let another person know you are
approaching. /amɛ̃e/ lets you know that it is all right to enter.
If the person inside does not wish you to enter, he will probably
answer /dąąbı/, 'no'. /agʋʋ/ is also used to ask for the attention
of a group or crowd. The response /amɛ̃e/ then means 'Speak, I'm
listening'.

2. /ɔ/ followed by /u/ becomes /o/, e.g., /mpó mũ/ is /mpó mũ/,
but is //mpɔ mu//.

3. Fufu is boiled and mashed yams or plantains which is served
with soup, /ŋkwãɲ/. Ampesı is boiled and diced yams or plantains
which is served with a stew, /ąbomũu/.

4. One of the ways of forming noun plurals is changing ɛ- to m-
or n-.

        ɛpó   joint   mpó   joints

        ɛdá   day   nná   days

49

5. The progressive tenses are formed by lengthening the vowel of the pronoun.

mẽyέ	I make	°mẽeyέ	I'm making
mẽká	I speak	°mẽeká	I'm speaking

In the regular orthography, the long vowel in the progressive is not written; instead ∥-re-∥ is written, as is spoken in the Akuapım dialect, e.g., /mẽeká/ is written ∥mereka∥. An Ashanti speaker may also say /mẽrẹká/ sometimes. The /rẹ-/ form is often used when there is a noun subject, but /εε-/ is more common.

6. /u/ followed by vowels other than /a/ is short and sounds somewhat like /w/, e.g., /mṹ εε/.

7. /εε/, which is ∥ε∥, means 'what about', 'as to', 'concerning' in sentences where there is no verb. With a verb, it has an adverbial or subordinating function. See Unit 9, note 1.

8. Adjectives are reduplicated for intensity, i.e., all or some part of the word is repeated. For monosyllabic stems, the most common form is with a long middle vowel, e.g., /pápaapa/, 'very good'.

9. The consecutive form, /á ~ ạ́/ plus simple stem, is <u>not</u> used after /pε/. 'I want him to go.' is /Mẽpε séὲ okó/, literally 'I want that he go'.

10. To show degree of comparison corresponding to English adjective plus '-er' or '-est', Twi employs the verb /sẽñ/, 'to move along', 'to surpass'. If you ask a native speaker of Twi to translate /sẽñ/, he will probably say it means 'than'. There are two basic constructions using /sẽñ/: (1) /sẽñ/ plus or minus an object after a preceeding verb, and (2) /sẽñ/ with an object, as the verb of the sentence. Compare the examples below.

/kyẽñ/, 'to surpass', 'excel', is also used in the same way to express comparison.

(1)

    (a)   Ɔwarę.   He ıs tall.

     Ɔwárę sɛ̃́.   He ıs taller.

     Ɔwárǫ sɛn nɪ́ n̆ǘą.   He ıs taller than hıs brother.

     Ɔwárę sɛn nɪ́ n̆yɪ̃n̆áa. He ıs the tallest.

    (b)   Eyé duru.   It ıs heavy.

     Eyé duru sɛ̃́.   It ıs heavıer.

     Eyé duru sɛ̃́ búùku nɔ̃́. It ıs heavıer than the book.

     Eyé duru sɛn nɪ́ n̆yɪ̃n̆áa. It ıs the heavıest of all.

(2)

    (a)   Ɔsɛn nɪ́ n̆ǘą pą̃́n̆yɪ̃́n̆.   He ıs older than hıs brother.
               ('He surpasses hıs brother
                ın age.')

    (b)   Ɔsɛn nɪ́ nuą nɔ́ wɔ ądesṹą́ He ıs better educated than
     mṹ.   hıs brother. ('He sur-
                passes hıs brother ın
                learnıng.')

New words

    warę   to be tall, long

    n̆yɪ̃n̆áa   all

    duru   heavy

    ɔpą̃́n̆yɪ̃́n̆ (pl. m-)   adult, old person, person
               of rank; old, agęd

    ądesṹą́   learnıng, study, educatıon

11. /adéɛ/, 'thing', plus a verb stem is a very productive type of compound, i.e., it can be used to form many new words, e.g., /adéɛ/ plus /súá/, 'to learn' gives /ạdesúá/, 'learning'.

12. /yé/ has an alternate form /yó/, which is fairly common in Ashanti, but /yó/ will not be understood by some speakers outside the Ashanti area.

    Lexical Drill A

1.	Ɛdɛ̧ɛ̃n na óoyɛ?	What is she doing?
2.	Ɛdɛ̧ɛ̃n na wóoyɛ?	What are they doing?
3.	Ɛdɛ̧ɛ̃n na wóoyɛ?	What are you doing?
4.	Ɛdɛ̧ɛ̃n na móoyɛ?	What are you (pl.) doing?
5.	Ɛdɛ̧ɛ̃n na wúudi?	What are you eating?
6.	Ɛdɛ̧ɛ̃n na wóoton?	What are they selling?
7.	Ɛdɛ̧ɛ̃n na móotɔ?	What are you (pl.) buying?
8.	Ɛdɛ̧ɛ̃n na óonóm?	What is he drinking?
9.	Ɛdɛ̧ɛ̃n na wóohwɛ?	What are they looking at?
10.	Ɛdɛ̧ɛ̃n na wóohwɛhwɛ?	What are you searching for?

    Lexical Drill B

1.	Ạfèi na óodidi.	Now he is eating.
2.	Ạfèi na wóodidi.	Now they are eating.
3.	Ạfèi na míidi.	Now I am eating.
4.	Ạfèi na yéedidi.	Now we are eating.
5.	Ạfèi na míidi ạkùtú.	Now I am eating an orange.
6.	Ạfèi na wóoton nsã́	Now they are selling palm wine.

    See Unit 18 notes 5 and 6 for discussion of secondary tones as in Lexical Drill B.

7. Ą́fèɪ na ɣɛ́ɛtɔ bankyɛ́.   We are now buying cassava.

8. Ą́fèɪ na ɔ́onɔ́m °sęgarɛ̀ɛtę.   He is now smoking a cigarette.

9. Ą́fèɪ na wɔ́ɔhwɛ °osęram̄́.   They are now looking at the moon.

10. Ą́fèɪ na mɛ́ehwǫ̀hwɛ mɛ́ pɛ̀n. I'm now looking for my pen.

New words

dɪ́	to employ, use, eat, spend, consume
dɪdɪ́	to eat
tɔ́ǹ	to buy
tɔ́	to sell
nɔ́m	to drink, smoke tobacco
hwęhwɛ́	to look for, search
ą́fèɪ, afèɪ	now
ąkutú	orange
nsɛ́	palm wine, alcoholic beverage
°sęgarɛ́ɛtę, sę́gàrɛtę.	cigarette
°osęram̄́ (pl. a-)	moon, month
pɛ́n (pɛ́n)	pen

Lexical Drill C

1. Ɔwárę sɛ̄n nɪ́ ñúa̯ ñɔ́.   He is taller than his brother.

2. Nɜ̃ hɔ́ yɛ́ dɛ̃́ñ sɛ̄n nɪ́   He is stronger than his brother.
   ñúa̯ ño.

3. Nɛ̃ hɔ́ yɛ́ fɛ sɛ̄n nɪ́   She is prettier than her sister.
   ñúa̯ nɔ́.

4. Ɔnóá fufúo sɛn ní ñúą She cooks fufu better than
   nó. her sister.

5. Ɔpɛ ampesíe sɛn ní ñúą He likes ampesie better than
   nó. his brother.

6. Ɔpɛ ądıdıądídì sɛn ní He likes to eat better than
   ñúą nó. his brother.

7. Ɔyɛ́ ądwùma sɛn ní ñúą He works better than his
   nó. brother.

8. Ɔwo sıká sɛn ní ñúą nó. He has more money than his
   brother.

9. Ɔwo nnéɛma sɛn ní ñúą He has more things than his
   nó. brother.

10. Ɔsó sɛn ní ñúą nó. He is bigger than his brother.

New words

fɛ   pretty, nice, beautiful

sıká   gold, money

só   to be big, large, much; to
                                reach, arrive at

ądıdéɛ   use, enjoyment, benefit

ądıdıądídì   enjoyment of eating a food

adéɛ (déɛ) (pl. nnéɛma)   thing, part

Lexical Drill D

1. Mɛ̃ káà nɔ̃́ sↄ̃ sɛ̃n wↄ́   My car is bigger than yours.
    dɛ̨́ɛ nↄ̃́.

2. Mɛ̃ hↄ̃́mà̃ yɛ fófóro sɛ̃n   My book is newer than yours.
    wↄ́ dɛ̨ɛ nↄ̃́.

3. Mɛ̃ hↄ̃́mà̃ yɛ fófóro sɛ̃n   My book is newer than his.
    nɛ̃́ dɛ̨ɛ nↄ̃́.

4. Wú akↄ̃ññúá̧ yɛ dɛ̃ñ sɛ̃n   Your chair is stronger than
    nɛ̃́ dɛ̨́ɛ nↄ̃́.   his.

5. Wú akↄ̃ññúá̧ yɛ dɛ̃ñ sɛ̃n   Your chair is stronger than
    mɛ̃́ dɛ̨ɛ nↄ̃́.   mine.

6. Nɛ̃́ dã̃ñ nↄ̃́ bↄ̨́ↄ yɛ dɛ̃ñ   His house is more expensive
    sɛ̃n mɛ̃ dɛ̨́ɛ nↄ̃́.   than mine.

7. Nↄ̃́ dã̃ñ nↄ̃́ bↄ̨́ↄ yɛ dɛ̃̀ñ   His house is more expensive
    sɛ̃n yɛ dɛ̨́ɛ nↄ̃́.   than ours.

8. Nɛ̃́ káà nↄ̃́ bↄ̨́ↄ yɛ °fↄ̨   His car costs less than mine.
    sɛ̃n mɛ̃́ dɛ̨́ɛ nↄ̃́.

9. Nɛ̃́ káà nↄ̃́ bↄ̨́ↄyɛ °fↄ̨   His car costs less than yours.
    sɛ̃n mↄ̃́ dɛ̨́ɛ nↄ̃́.

10. Mɛ̃́ pénsɛ̀rɛ̨ nↄ̃́ yɛ́ sɛ̃n   My pencil is better than yours.
    mↄ̃́ dɛ̨́ɛ nↄ̃́.

New words

ŋhómã̃ (hómã̃) (pl. °ŋgómã̃)	skin, hide; vellum; book, letter; leather
fófǫrǫ	new, another
ɔdã́ñ (dã́ñ) (pl. n-~a-)	house, room, building
ɛbǫ́ǫ (pl. m-)	price; stone, pit, seed
°fǫ	cheap, plenty, plentiful

Lexical Drill E

1. Ɔdã́ñ yí mú suą sɛñ baakó nó.

   This room is smaller than that one.

2. Kanęa yí hyęrɛñ sɛñ baakó nó.

   This light is brighter than the other one.

3. Ɔkwã́ñ yí yɛ sɛñ baakó nó.

   This road is better than that one.

4. Ąkóñ̃ñúą yí yɛ fǫ sɛñ baakó nó.

   This chair is cheaper than that one.

5. Ŋhómã̃ yí mú yɛ duru sɛñ baakó nó.

   This book is heavier than that one.

New words in drills

emú (pl. a-)	whole, entirety
suą	to be small, few
eyí	this, these
baakó	one

hyɛrɛ́ñ   to penetrate, get through,
                                shine

ɔkwáñ (pl. ṇ-)   road, path, way

Lexical Drill F

1. Nęa ɛwɔ hɛ́ na ɛyɛ́ fọ?   Which one is cheaper?
2. Nęa ɛwɔ hɛ́ na ɛyɛ́?   Which one is better?
3. Nęa ɛwɔ hɛ́ na ɛbɛ́kyɛ?   Which one will last longer?
4. Nęa ɛwɔ hɛ́ na ɛyɛ́ dɛ́ñ?   Which one is harder?
5. Nęa ɛwɔ hɛ́ na ɛwɔ   Which one is stronger?
   ahɔ̆ɔdɛ́ñ?

Now words

        kyɔ   to last, endure; divide
                            separate, share

        ahɔ̆ɔdę́ṇ   .strength, (literally 'body
                            hard')

        nęa   he who, that which, he whose,
                            where

        ahɛ́   how much, how many, how long

Pattern Drill A

1. Ɛdę́ɛn na wọ́pὲ sɛ́ɛ́ wúdı?   What would you like to eat?
2. Ɛdę́ɛn na wọ́pὲ sɛ́ɛ́ wọ́hwɛ? What would you like to see?
3. Ɛdę́ɛn na wọ́pὲ sɛ́ɛ́ wọ́tɔ? What would you like to buy?
4. Ɛdę́ɛn na wọ́pὲ sɛ́ɛ́   What would you like to read?
   wọ́kɛñkáñ?
5. Ɛdę́ɛn na wọ́pὲ sɛ́ɛ́ wọ́nõm? What would you like to drink?

57

Pattern Drill B

1. Mɛ̄pɛ sɛ́ɛ̀ mĩ́dí ạkwạdú.	I'd like to eat a banana.
2. Mɛ̄pɛ sɛ́ɛ̀ mɛ̄hwɛ́ Ghánà.	I'd like to see the University
Únìversɪty nɔ̃́.	of Ghana.
3. Mɛ̄pɛ sɛ́ɛ̀ mɛ̄tó mpabọá.	I'd like to buy some shoes.
4. Mɛ̄pɛ sɛ́ɛ̀ mĩ́kã̃́ɲ ɳ̀hómã̀.	I'd like to read a book.
5. Mɛ̄pɛ sɛ́ɛ̀ mɛ̄nóm nsã́.	I'd like to drink palm wine.

New words

kã̃́ɲ	to count, read
kɛ̃̄ɲkã̃́ɲ	to read, count
ạkwạdú (pl. ɳ-)	banana
mpabọá (mpábọ̀a)	shoe, pair of shoes

13. /ɛdę̃́ɲ/ is a contraction and alternate form of /ɛdę́ɛ bɛ̃̄ɲ/,
'what thing'. /bɛ̃̄ɲ/ is 'what', 'which', 'what kind of'.

14. In statements if /dɪ/ is not followed by the name of some
food, it is necessary to say /dɪdí/ for clarity and propriety
because /mĩ́dɪ/ can mean 'I eat' or 'I have sexual relations with'.

15. /ạ́fèɪ/ may also occur at the end of an utterance, but in
response to a question like /ɛdę̃́n na ɔ́ɔyɛʔ/ you must use /ạ́fèɪ
na/ at the beginning of the response if /ạ́fèɪ/ is used.

16. Stative verbs like /pɛ/ and /wɔ/ have low tone. Other
monosyllabic verbs have. high tone in the present tenses.

17. /sę̄garɛ́ɛ̀tę/ is //cigarette//.
/ɔsę̄ram̃́/ is //ɔsram//.

18. For explanation of /ampesíe/ and /fufúo/, see Unit 9.

19. /fǫ/ is // fow//.

20. /adéɛ/ does not refer to persons. To compare persons, you must use two nouns, e.g., 'My child is taller than yours', is /Mɛ̃ bá wárę sɛ̃ñ wǫ bá/.

21. /baakɔ̃ nɔ̃/ means 'the second one', 'the other one', as opposed to the one previously mentioned.

22. Phrases, like those with /mṹ/, such as /ɔdã̃ñ yí mṹ/, 'the whole of this room', 'this room's entirety', are nominal phrases and function in a sentence in the same manner as any single-stem or compound noun. In this type of construction, the second noun (which indicates place or location) is always high-toned and never loses its vowel. For example, /mṹ/ is always /mṹ/ after a phrasal compound, but it may be /-m̀/ after a single-stem or compound noun. See also Unit 4, note 17.

   Possession in nouns is marked by word order. The first noun is the possessor, the second, the possessed. If the first noun has modifiers other than possessive pronouns, they will occur between the two nouns, e.g., /nɛ̃ dã̃ñ nɛ̃ bǫ́o/, 'his house's price', 'the price of his house', literally 'his structure that one seed'.

23. /ŋgɔ̃mã̃/ is // nhoma//. /ɲhɔ̃mã̃/ has a number of plurals: /ŋgɔ̃mã̃/, /ahɔ̃mã̃/, /ɲhɔ̃mã̃/. These are dialectal or regional variants.

24. It is VERY IMPORTANT to eat only with the RIGHT hand. The left hand is for toilet functions only. Do not hand another person anything with the left hand. Do not wave at anyone with the left hand.

25. Verbs have secondary tones after /na/. See Unit 18, note 5. Conjunctions which are followed by secondary tones are also followed by /,/. The /,/ is not written in this manual, as in the orthography, since it is predictable.

Unit 7

Basic Dialogue

-A-

kó, kɔ	to go, go away
°sɔ́tɔɔ̀	store

1 Méko °sɔ́tɔɔ̀ mṹ ɔkyɛ́nã́.   I will go to the store tomorrow.

-B-

2 Wɔ́ɔ̀kɔtó dɛ̀ɛ́ñ?   What are you going to buy?

-A-

ạduạnɛ́ (pl. n-)	food

3 Mɛ̃ekɔtó ạduạnɛ́.   I'm going to buy food.

-B-

4 Ạduạnɛ́ bɛ́n na wɔ́ɔ̀kɔtó?   What kind of food are you going to buy?

-A-

nsúo, nsú	water
ɛnám	meat, flesh
nsuomnám	fish

5 Mɛ̃ekɔtó nsuomnám   I'm going to buy fish.

-B-

ɛhɛ́ (pl. ɛ-nṍm)	where
ɔfá (fá) (pl. ạfũạfá)	half, piece; other side, other part
tóɲ̀	to sell

6 Ɛhɛ́fá na yɛtɔ́n nsuomnám   Where do they sell good fish?
   pápa?

-A-

   °Kíñswèı   Kıngsway super market

7 °Kíñswèı na ɛtɔ́n nám pá.   Kıngsway sells good fish.

-B-

8 Na nsuomnám bɔ́o yɛ dɛ̃ñ   Is fish expensive?
   anáa?

-A-

   mmɛrɛ   cheap

9 Dąąbí, nám nɔ́ bɔ́o yɛ mmɛrɛ.   No, fish ıs cheap.

Notes

1. Twı (like English) uses /kɔ/ 'go' as an auxılıary verb (1)
for an ımmedıate future and (2) to express purpose. For example
/Mɪ́ıkodıdí/ can mean eıther (1) 'I am goıng relatıvely soon to
eat' or (2) 'I am goıng for the purpose of eatıng'. The fırst
syllable of the verb followıng /kɔ/ has hıgh tone; the other
syllables have the same tone as the present stem. The future
/médıdı/, 'I wıll eat', ıs a proxımate future. The ımplıcatıon
of the proxımate future ıs that the tıme referred to ıs more
ındefınıte and/or further ın the future than that referred to by
an ımmedıate future. Auxılıary /kɔ/ ıs always ın the progressıve.

2. /sɔ́tɔɔ̀/ ıs // store//. /ąguądídáñ/, 'tradıng house', ıs also
common. /ąguá̧/ ıs 'market', 'market place', /dı ąguá̧/ ıs 'to
trade', 'deal ın'.

3. One of the characterıstıcs of Ashantı Twı ıs an /ɛ/ at the end
of many words whıch end ın a nasal ın other dıalects, e.g.,
/ąduąnɛ́/. Consequently, ın prınted texts both // aduan// and

61

// aduane// will occur.

4. A schwa (a sound like the second vowel in English 'sofa') usually occurs between an /m/ and an /n/, as in /nsuomnám/.

5. /ɛhɛ́/ and /ɛhɛ́fá/ can be used interchangeably.

6. /Kíñsẅeı/ is // Kıngsway//.

7. Locatıve nomınals like /ɛhɛ́/ and /ɛhá/ have a dıstrıbutıve plural. /ɛhɛ́nõm/ means 'whereabouts', /ɛhánõm/, 'hereabouts', 'ın thıs general vıcınıty'.

8. /ɔfá/ has an alternate form /ɛfá/.

Pattern Drıll A

1.	Mɛ́kɔ sɔ́tɔɔ̀ mú ɔkyɛ́na.	I wıll go to the store tomorrow.
2.	<u>Médı fufúo ɔkyɛ́nã.</u>	<u>I wıll eat fufu</u> tomorrow.
3.	<u>Métɔ °bɔrɔdɔ ɔkyɛ́nã.</u>	<u>I wıll buy bread</u> tomorrow.
4.	<u>Ɔbɛ́ba há ɔkyɛ́nã.</u>	<u>He wıll come here</u> tomorrow.
5.	<u>Ɔbɛ́ba há fırı Kumásɛ</u> ɔkyɛ́nã.	<u>He wıll come here from Kumase</u> tomorrow.
6.	<u>Wobɛ́kɔ Ŋkɛrã́ñ ɔkyɛ́nã.</u>	<u>They wıll go to Accra</u> tomorrow.
7.	<u>Wobétu áfìrı Ŋkɛrã́ñ</u> ɔkyɛ́nã.	<u>They wıll leave from Accra</u> tomorrow.
8.	<u>Yɛbétoñ yɛɳ káà nɔ́</u> ɔkyɛ́nã.	<u>We wıll sell our car</u> tomorrow.

9. Yebédɪ nsuomnám   We will eat fish tomorrow.
   ɔkyéná.

10. Ɛhɛ́fá na méhū wɔ ɔkyéná?   Where will you be tomorrow?
                              ('Where I will see you
                              tomorrow?')

Pattern Drill B

1. Mɛ́eŋkɔ́ sɔ́toɔ̀ mú ɔkyéná.   I will not go to the store
                                 tomorrow.

2. Mɛ́ɛnnɪ fufúo ɔkyéná.   I will not eat fufu tomorrow.

3. Mɛ́ɛntɔ́ bɔrɔdɔ ɔkyéná.   I will not buy bread tomorrow.

4. Ɔ̀ɔmmá há ɔkyéná.   He will not come here tomorrow.

5. Ɔ̀ɔmmá há mfɪrí Kumásɛ   He will not come here from
   ɔkyéná.   Kumase tomorrow.

6. Wáɔ̀ŋkɔ́ Ŋkɛɾáñ ɔkyéná.   They will not go to Accra
                               tomorrow.

7. Wóɔ̀mmá mfɪrí Ŋkɛɾáñ   They will not leave from Accra
   ɔkyéná.   tomorrow.

8. Yɛ́ɛmmá wo fíe ɔkyéná.   We won't come to your house
                               tomorrow.

9. Mɔ́ɔ̀mmá sukúù ɔkyéná.   You (pl.) won't be at school
                               tomorrow.

10. Mɛ́ɛntumí ŋkɔ́ ɔkyéná.   I won't be able to go tomorrow.

Pattern Drill C

1.	Ɛhɛ́fá na wóokɔ?	Where are they going?
2.	Wɔɔkɔ́ sɔ́tɔɔ̀ mú.	They are going to the store.
3.	Wɔɔkɔtɔ́ ạkutú wɔ sɔ́tɔɔ̀ mú.	They are going to buy oranges at the store.
4.	Wɔɔkɔtɔ́ ạkutú wɔ Kíñswèı.	They are going to buy oranges at Kingsway's.
5.	Yɛtɔ́ŋ nsuomnám pápa. wɔ Kíñswèı.	They sell good fish at Kingway's.
6.	Yɛtɔ́ŋ nsuomnám pápa wɔ Ŋkɛrã́ñ.	They sell good fish at Accra.
7.	Mífırı Ŋkɛrạ́ñ.	I am from Accra.
8.	Mífırı Kumásẹ.	I am from Kumasi.
9.	Métu ạ́fìrı Kumásẹ.	I will move from Kumasi.
10.	Métu ạ́fìrı há.	I will move from here.

Pattern Drill D

1.	Mɛ̃́ekotɔ́ fíe wɔ Koforíduà.	I'm going to buy a house at Koforidua.
2.	Mɛ̃́ekotɔ́ŋ fíe wɔ Koforíduà.	I'm going to sell a house at Koforidua.
3.	Mɛ̃́ekotɔ́ŋ nsuomnám yí.	I'm going to sell these fish.
4.	Mɛ̃́ekofá nsuomnám yí.	I'm going to take these fish.
5.	Mɛ̃́ekofá ní sıká ámà nɔ̃́.	I'm going to take the money to him.

6. Mḯ₁kogyá sıká nŏ ámá.   I'm going to leave the money
    nŏ.   for him.

7. Mḯ₁kogyá nŏ wo fíe.   I'm going to leave her at
                               home.

8. ᵒMẽekɔsɛrá nŏ wo fíe.   I'm to visit him at home.

9. Mẽekɔsɛrá mẽ papá.   I'm going to visit my father.

10. Mḯ₁kohṹ mẽ papá.   I'm going to see my father.

New words

        fa   to take, take away, sieze,
                           obtain, get; up to, as far as;
                           by means of; about, concerning

        gyą̈   to leave, quit, forsake; send
                           away; accompany

       ᵒsɛrá   to visit; smear, grease

Question and Answer Drill A

1. Ɛdɛ́n na óokã̃ñkã̃́ñ?   What is he reading?

    Ookã́ñ nhŏmã áà ɛfá   He is reading a book about

    Ghánà hŏ.   Ghana.

2. Ɛdɛ́n fufúo na wopɛ?   What kind of fufu do they like?

    Wopɛ bɔrɔdɛ́ɛ fufúo.   They like plaintain fufu.

3. Ɛhɛ́rá na yɛtó̀ɲ mpabɔá? Where do they sell shoes?

    Yɛtó̀ɲ mpabɔá wɔ sɔ́tɔɔ̀   They sell shoes at the store.

    mṹ.

65

4. Obédɪ nná ahé?

How long will he be here?
('He will consume days how
many?')

    Obédɪ ɔsɛram̄ wɔ há.

He will spend a month here.

5. Wɔ̀bɛká̄ ákyɛ̀rɛ́ nɔ̄ sɛ́ɛ̀
    mɛ̃wɔ há?

Will you tell him I am here?

    Áàñ, mɛ́ká̄ ákyɛ̀rɛ́ nɔ̄
    sɛ́ɛ̀ wɔ́wɔ̀ há?

Yes, I will tell him you
are here.

New Words

        ɔdɛ́ɛ

yam

        bɔrodɛ́ɛ

plaintain, 'European yam'

        áà

which, that, what, where

Question and Answer Drill B

1. Ɛdɛ̣ɛ̃ñ ạduạnɛ́ na wɔ́pɛ̀ dí?

What do you like to eat?

    Mɛ̃pɛ akotúdɪe.

I like to eat oranges.
('I like orange-eating.')

2. Ɛdɛ̣ɛ̃ñ na wɔ́pɛ̀ yɛ́?

What do you like to do?

    Mɛ̃pɛ sɪnííìko.

I like to go to the movies.

3. Ɛdɛ̣ɛ̃ñ na wɔ́pɛ̀ nsá̃nõm?

What do you like to drink?

    Mɛ̃pɛ nsá̃nõm.

I like to drink palm wine.

4. Ɛdeɛ́n na wópè yɛ?   What do you like to do?

    Mɛ̃pɛ <u>anansɛsɛmkã́</u>.   I like to tell fairy tales.

                                    ('I like spider story

                                    telling.')

5. Ɛdeɛ́n na wópè kɔrá?   What do you like to save?

    Mɛ̃pɛ <u>sɪkákɔ̀rá</u>.   I like to save money.

Pattern Drill E

1. Kã́ kyɛrɛ́ nõ sɛ́ɛ̀ ɛwo   Tell him that it is here.
    há.

2. <u>Bɪsa</u> nõ sɛ́ɛ̀ ɛwo há.   Ask him if it is here.

3. Bɪsa nõ <u>sɛ́ɛ̀ ɔkó anã́a</u>.   Ask him if he is gone.

4. <u>Hwɛ́</u> sɛ́ɛ̀ ɔkó anã́a.   See if he is gone.

5. Hwɛ́ sɛ́ɛ̀ owo há anã́a.   See if he is here.

6. <u>Wúnɪ̀m</u> sɛ́ɛ̀ owo há anã́a? Do you know if he is here?

7. Wúnɪ̀m <u>nea</u> owɔ?   Do you know where it is?

8. <u>Onnɪ́m</u> nea owɔ.   He doesn't know where he is.

9. Onnɪ́m nea ɛwɔ.   He doesn't know where it is.

10. <u>Bɪsa</u> nõ nea ɛwɔ.   Ask him where it is.

New words

    sɛ́ɛ̀ . . . anã́a   if, whether

    nɪ̃m   to know, know how

9. /bɔrɔdɔ̦/ is // brodo//. Another common word for bread is
/páàno̦/.

10. /Mɪ̃fɪrɪ Kumásɛ̦/ is 'I am from Kumasi', i.e., 'Kumasi is my
home town'. /Mɪ̃fɪrɪ́ Kumásɛ̦ na mɛ̃ebá/ is 'I am coming from Kumasi'.

11. If a subject has two verbs, both verbs have the negative
prefix if the sentence is negative, e.g., /Wómmá m̲firí Kumásę/,
'They won't leave from Kumasi'.

12. The negative of the present progressive is also the negative
of the future, e.g., /Mę́ęŋkó/ corresponds to both 'I am not going'
and 'I will not go'. /Mę́ęŋkó/ is // Merenko//.

13. /sęrá/ is // sra//.

14. First person plural impersonal often corresponds to English
third person plural impersonal, e.g., /Yɛtóŋ̀/, 'they sell'.
Compare Pattern Drill C, sentences 5 and 6.

15. /mã/, 'to give', 'cause', when the second verb with a subject
often corresponds to an English indirect object or benefactive
prepositional phrase, i.e., it translates 'to', 'for', 'on the
behalf of', 'for the benefit of'. For example, /Mę́ękɔfá ní siká
ámà nó/, 'I'm going to take him the money', 'I'm going to take
the money to give /it/ to him'.

16. You can only /sęrá/, 'to visit', a person. You /hwɛ/, 'to
look at', 'observe' a building or place. You can /hũ/, 'to see',
'visit', a person, building, or place.

17. Verbs without objects are often reduplicated for clarity or
specification, e.g., /kã́ñ/ is 'to read', 'count'; /kã́ñ ŋhɔ́mã/ is
'to read a book'; /kẽñkã́ñ/ without an object usually means 'to
read'. See Question and Answer Drill A, sentence one.

18. An English noun followed by a prepositional phrase corresponds
in Twi to a noun plus a subordinate clause, e.g., /nhɔ́mã áà ɛfá
Ghánà hɔ́/, 'a book about Ghana', 'a book which is about Ghana',
literally 'book which takes hold of Ghana's self'.

19.   Habitual desires or preferences are expressed by the simple
stem following /pɛ/, 'to like'. Stems ending in /-ɪ/ have an
alternate form ending in /-ɪe/, e.g., /dɪ ~ dɪe/.

20.   In Ghanian folklore the spider is a wily, crafty fellow who
nevertheless often gets the worse of a bargain or situation.

21.   Compound nouns are formed in several ways. In some compounds,
the first noun has the same tone(s) as in isolation and the second
noun has the same tone(s) as when following a possessive pronoun.
Compare Unit 6 note 22. In other compounds, the first noun has
all low tones and the second the same tone(s) as in isolation,
e.g., /nsúom̀ nám/ is /nsuomnám/.

22.   /áà/ is /à/.

69

Unit 8

Basic Dialogue

-A-

yarɛ́	to be ill, sick
sa	to cure
ɔyarɛsáfʠɔ (pl. a-)	physician

1　Ɔyarɛsáfʠɔ nɔ̃ wɔ hɔ́ anã̄a?　Is the doctor in?

-B-

2　Ą̃ą̃ñ, ɔyarɛsáfʠɔ nɔ̃ wɔ hɔ́.　Yes, the doctor is in.

-C-

amannɛ́ɛ (amánnɛ̧́ɛ)	message, mission

3　Wamánnɛ̧́ɛ?　What's the matter? Why have you come? ('Your mission?')

-A-

4　Mɛ̃ntɛ̧́ ápɔ̀.　I don't feel well.

-C-

°ɛyá	pain, ache; grief, distress

5　Wɔ hɛ́fã na ɛyɛ́ wɔ °yá?　Where do you hurt? ('Your where half then is your pain?')

-A-

etí, etírı (pl. ą-)	head

6　Mĩ tí yɛ́ mɛ̃ yá.　My head hurts.

yą̃m̀	the insides of the body

7　Mĩ yą̃m̀ ńsʠ yɛ́ mɛ̃ yá.　My stomach hurts too.

70

-C-

gyɛ   to take, receive, accept,
                                                 take internally

ạdúru (pl. n-)   medicine

8 ᵒGyı ạdúru yí.   Take this medicine.

Notes

1. /-fɔ́ɔ/, which is //-fo//, corresponds to English (1) '-er'
which forms agent nouns from verbs, e.g., /ɔyarɛsáfɔ̀ɔ/,
'diseasecurer', 'physician', and (2) '-er' or '-an' meaning 'the
people of', 'the inhabitants of', e.g., /Ŋkɛráñfɔ́ɔ/, 'the people
of Accra'. /-fɔ́ɔ/ occurs (a) with both the singular and plural
of some stems, (b) with only the plural of some stems, having
/-ní/ with the singular, and (c) with both the singular and plural,
having /-ní/ as an alternate form with the singular. This type
of noun has an /ɔ- ~ o-/ prefix in the singular and an /a- ~ ạ-/
prefix in the plural. Sometimes /n-/ also occurs with the plural.
/ɔyarɛsáfɔ̀ɔ/, 'doctor', has an alternate form /ɔyarɛsɛ́nı/.
/ayarɛsáfɔ̀ɔ/, 'doctors', has an alternate form /ñyarɛsáfɔ̀ɔ/.
/ɔsáfɔɔ/, 'dancer' and /osɛ́nı/, 'warrior', both have the plural
/asáfɔɔ/.

2. /ɛyá/ is // ɛyaw//. Ashanti dialect usually has a final vowel
where Akuapım dialect has a vowel plus /-w/, as in /ɛyáw/.

3. /Gyı ạdúru yí/ is // Gye aduru yı//. Vowel harmony agreement
will not be footnoted after this unit. Review vowel harmony
rules in Unit 2.

Lexical Drill A

1. Mĩ tí yɛ́ mɛ̃ yá.	My head hurts.
2. Mĩ y̧ắm̀ yɛ́ mɛ̃ yá.	My stomach hurts.
3. Mɛ́ nsá yɛ́ mɛ̃ yá.	My hand hurts.
4. Mɛ̃ nắñ yɛ́ mɛ̃ yá.	My foot hurts.
5. ᵒM̧akyí yɛ́ mɛ̃ yá.	My back hurts.
6. ᵒM̧ab̧atí yɛ́ mɛ̃ yá.	My shoulder hurts.

Pattern Drill A

1. Wamánnę̇ɛ.	What's your problem?
2. Namánnę̇ɛ.	What's his problem?
3. M̧óàmánnę̇ɛ.	What's your (pl.) problem?
4. Wón amánnę̇ɛ.	What's their problem?
5. Yamánnę̇ɛ.	What's our problem?

New Words

nsá	hand, arm
ɛnắñ	foot, leg
ąkyí	the back, rear; back, behind
ab̧átɪ, b̧atírɪ (b̧àtì) (pl. m-)	shoulder

Pattern Drill B

1. Mɛ̃hṹ.	I see it.
2. Mɛ̃hṹ nő.	I see him.
3. Mɛ̃ehwęhwɛ́ nő.	I'm looking for him.
4. Mɛ̃ehwęhwɛ́ ɔyarę̧sáfǫ́ɔ nő.	I'm looking for the doctor.
5. Kohṹ ɔyarę̧sáfǫ́ɔ nő.	Go see the doctor.

6. Kohũ nõ sɛ́ɛ́ ɔpɛ biribí   Go see <u>if he wants some-</u>
    ą̃dì.   <u>thing to eat.</u>

7. Bisa nõ sɛ́ɛ́ ɔpɛ biribí   <u>Ask</u> him <u>if he wants some-</u>
    ą̃dì.   <u>thing to eat.</u>

8. Bisa nõ <u>sɛ́ɛ́ nɛ̃ hɛ́fá na</u>   Ask him <u>where he hurts.</u>
    <u>ɛyɛ nɛ̃ yá.</u>

9. H̀wɛ́ sɛ́ɛ́ nɛ̃ hɛ́fá na ɛyɛ   <u>See</u> where he hurts.
    nɛ̃ yá.

10. Hwɛ́ <u>sɛ́ɛ́ ɔpɛ ŋhómã̌ átɔ̀.</u>   See <u>if he wants to buy a</u>
                                 <u>book.</u>

New word

       biribí   something, anything, nothing
                             (in negative sentences)

Question and Answer Drill A

1. Ɔyarɛsáfɔ́ɔ nõ wɔ há?   Is the doctor in?
    <u>Dą̀ąbí</u>, ɔyarɛsáfɔ́ɔ nõ   <u>No</u>, the doctor isn't in.
    nní há.

2. Ɛhɛ́fá na ɔyarɛsáfɔ́ɔ nõ   Where is the doctor?
    wɔ?
       Ɔyarɛsáfɔ́ɔ nõ <u>wɔ</u>   The doctor <u>is at the</u>
       ayarɛsábɛ̀a hó.   <u>hospital.</u>

3. Ɔyaresáfɔ́ɔ nõ wɔ ɔbɔáfɔ́ɔ   Does the doctor have an
    anáa?   assistant?
    Ą̀ą̃ń, owɔ ɔbɔáfɔ́ɔ.   <u>Yes, he has</u> an assistant.

4. Ɛdɛɛ́n ntí na wúukohǔ
   dókɛ̀ta nǒ?

   Mȋıkohǔ dókɛ̀ta esiá̰nɛ̀
   sɛ́ɛ̀ mēyarɛ̀.

   Why are you going to see the
   doctor?

   I'm going to see the doctor
   because I am sick.

5. Wɔ́pè sɛ́ɛ̀ mēbó wɔ páanɛ ɛ?

   Ą̰ą̰ñ, mēpɛ sɛ́ɛ̀ wɔ́bɔ mɛ̃
   páanɛ ɛ.

   Do you want me to give you a
   shot? ('You like that I
   strike you needle?')

   Yes, I want you to give me
   a shot.

6. Mmɔfára nǒ °rɛgɔrɔ́ wɔ
   sukúùdán nǒ mǔ?

   Dą̰ą̰bí, wɔɔgɔrɔ́ wɔ
   sukúùdán nǒ ą̰kyí.

   Are the children playing in
   the school building?

   No, they are playing behind
   the school building.

7. Mmɔfára nǒ rɛgɔrɔ́ wɔ
   agɔrɔ́bɛ̀a hó?

   Ą̰ą̰ñ, wɔɔgɔrɔ́ wɔ
   agɔrɔ́bɛ̀a hó?

   Are the children playing at
   the playground?

   Yes, they are playing at
   the playground.

8. Ɔyarɛsáfɔ́ɔ nǒ rıkohǔ
   abɔfára nǒ anǎa?

   Ą̰ą̰ñ, obéhǔ nǒ.

   Is the doctor going to see the
   child?

   Yes, he will see him.

9. Wɔ hó tɛ sɛ̃n nnɛ́?

   Mɛ̃ hó yɛ́ nnɛ́ sɛ̃n
   nnɛ́ra.

   How are you today?

   I feel better today than I
   did yesterday.

10. Wúbedı nná ahɛ̃ wo há?

    Médı ɔsɛram.

    How long will you be here?

    I will be here a month.

New words

bęá (bę́a) (pl. m-)	place; manner
ayaręsábęa (pl. ñ-)	hospital, clinic, doctor's office
bǫá	to help
ɔbǫáfǫ́ɔ (pl. a-)	helper, assistant
dókę̀ta	doctor
esiá̯nę̀	because, on account of
bɔ	to strike, hit, come in contact with; break, destroy; shoot
páanę ɛ (pl. m-)	needle
bɔ. . .páanę ɛ	to give a shot of medicine
gɔrǫ, goru	to play
agɔrǫ́bęa	place to play, playground
n̩l í	therefore, because
ɛdę ɛ̯n ntí	why

Lexical Drill B

1. Mẽpɛ sɛ́ɛ́ wǫ́ na wǫ́ká
   káà nǒ.

   I want YOU to drive the car.

2. Mẽpɛ <u>sɛ́ɛ́ onǒ</u> na ɔká̯
   <u>káà nǒ</u>.

   I want <u>HIM to drive the car</u>.

3. <u>Wɔpɛ sɛ́ɛ́ onǒ</u> na ɔká̯
   káà nǒ.

   <u>They want</u> HIM to drive the car.

4. Wɔpɛ <u>ñõmá̯kyęrɛ́w</u>.

   They like <u>to write letters</u>.

5. <u>Yɛpɛ</u> ñõmá̯kyęrɛ́w.

   <u>We like</u> to write letters.

75

6.	Yɛpɛ káàká.	We like _to drive a car._
7.	Ɔpɛ káàká.	He likes to drive a car.
8.	Ɔpɛ káà ákǎ.	He wants _a car to drive._
9.	Mɛ̃pɛ káà ákǎ.	_I want_ a car to drive.
10.	Mɛ̃pɛ fufúo ə̃dì.	I want _some fufu to eat._

Lexical Drill C

1.	Mĩtumí kǎ lórè̩.	I am able to drive a car.
2.	Mɛ̃ǹtumí ɲkǎ lórè̩.	_I can't_ drive a car.
3.	Mɛ̃ǹtumí ɲkó nné.	I can't _go today._
4.	Wòǹtumí ɲkó nné.	_They can't_ go today.
5.	Wòǹtumí ntè̩ wɔ mfí há.	They can't _hear you from here._
6.	Ɔyarè̩fɔɔ nǒ ntè̩ wɔ mfí há.	_The patient_ can't hear you from here.
7.	Ɔyarè̩fɔɔ nǒ pɛ bɪrɪbí ə̃kè̩nkə̃́ñ.	The patient _wants something to read._
8.	°Ɔbarè̩má nǒ pɛ bɪrɪbí ə̃kè̩nkə̃́ñ.	_The man_ wants something to read.
9.	Ɔbarè̩má nǒ béhũ ɔbáa nǒ ɔkyéna.	The man _will see the woman tomorrow._
10.	_Ayarè̩fɔɔ hwɛ́fɔò nǒ_ béhũ ɔbáa nǒ ɔkyéna.	_The nurse_ will see the woman tomorrow.

New words

ayarè̩fɔɔ (pl. a-)	patient, sick person, invalid
hwɛ́fɔɔ (pl. a-)	caretaker, supervisor

ayarɛ́fɔɔ hwɛ́fɔɔ (pl. ñ-)   nurse

ɔbarɛ́má (pl. m-)   man, male

ɔbáa (pl. m-)   woman, female

Pattern Drill C

1. Tó   Buy it.

2. Tó nṍ.   Buy him.

3. Tó ɛnɛ́.   Buy that one.

4. Tó bı.   Buy some.

5. Tó mã mɛ̃.   Buy it for me.

Pattern Drill D

1. Mɪ́po bı.   I want some.

2. Mã mɛ̃ bı.   Give me some

3. Fa mã mɛ̃.   Give it to me.

4. Fa ɛnɛ́ mã mɛ̃.   Give me that one.

5. Tó ɛnɛ́ mã mɛ̃.   Buy that one for me.

4.   Object pronouns have low tone unless emphatic. Singular
object pronouns at conversation speed sometimes occur with only
their consonant, ı.e., /mɛ̃, wɔ, nṍ/ may be low-toned verb suffixes
/-m̀, -ẁ, -ǹ/.

5.   /bɛá/, 'place', corresponds to English '-ry', place where,
e.g., /ayarɛsábɛ̀a/, 'place where curing is done', 'hospital',
'clinic'.
      /bɛá/, also means manner, as ın /nkɛ̀rábɛ̀a/, 'fate', 'destiny',

'manner of death', from /kẹrà/, 'to take leave of', 'bid farewell to '.

6. /gorǫ́/ is usually // goru//. In Akuapim it is /goru/.

7. To make the pronoun subject of a verb emphatic, an emphatic pronoun plus /na/ comes before the verb. The verb still has its pronoun subject prefix, e.g., /onố na ɔkấ/, 'HE drives'. The emphatic pronouns are:

mẽ	yέŋ
wǫ́	mố
onố	wɔ́ŋ
εnố	εnố

If a noun subject is emphatic, it is followed by /na/ and the verb has a pronoun subject prefix, singular or plural corresponding to the emphatic noun.

8. /ayarẹ́fɔɔ hwέfɔɔ/ also occurs as /ayarẹhwέfɔɔ/.

9. /ɔbarẹ̣́ma/ is // ɔbarima// and is often /ɔbaẹ̣́ma/. /ɔbarẹ̣́ma/, 'the male of the species', is used to form compound nouns, e.g., /oñű̦bárẹma/, 'male sibling', 'brother', and /ɔbábarẹma/, 'male child', 'son'.

10. /ɔbáa/ is /obẹ́a/ in Akuapim dialect. /ɔbáa/ is also used in compound nouns and means 'the female of the species'. Compare note 9.

Unit 9

Basic Dialogue

-A-

1 °Wạ̀kòdıdí anâa?   Have you gone to eat yet?

-B-

2 °Mínnıdííyε.   I haven't eaten yet.

-A-

3 εhếfá na yéŋkodídı?   Where shall we go to eat?
                                       (Where should we go to eat?)

-B-

4 M(ã̃) yεŋkó mĩ fíe.   Let's go to my house.

-A-

5 εdẹ̃́ñ na wọ́pè̀ sèέ wúdı nnê?   What would you like to eat today?

-B-

                nnéra   yesterday

6 Mĩdıı ampesíe nnéra.   I ate ampesı yesterday.

                entí   therefore

7 Entí m(ã̃) yεnní fufúo nnế.   So let's eat fufu today.

-A-

8 M(ã̃) yεŋkó ạ́fèı.   Let's go now.

-B-

                yọ̣ọ̣   yes, O.K.

9 Yọ̣ọ̣, m(ã̃) yεŋkó.   O.K., let's go.

79

Notes

1.   The transitive positive past tense is marked by the doubling
(or lengthening) of the last vowel, semi-vowel, or nasal, e.g.,
/hũu/, 'saw' (from /hũ/), /taáà/, 'chased' (from /taá/), /buéè/,
'opened', 'undid' (from /bué/), /tóǹǹ/, 'sold' (from /tóǹ/),
/kyɛ̨rɛ́wẁ/, 'wrote' (from /kyɛ̨rɛ́w/).
    The tone of the positive past tense ending is low, and the
tone of final stem vowel is high except as given below. (1) Monosyllabic stems have a low stem if followed by an object.   (2)
Verbs of motion and /hũ/, 'to see', have a low stem vowel with
and without a following object.   An intransitive suffix /-y/ is
added if there is no verb object, and a temporal adverbial suffix
/-ɛ/ also occurs after /-y/.   But some verbs never occur without
an expressed object.   /-yɛ/ is a freely alternating form of /-y/
for some (especially younger) speakers, but many speakers use
/-yɛ/ only in temporal clauses, e.g., /mɛ̃baay/, 'I came', and
/mɛ̃baayɛ/, 'when I came', are kept distinct by many persons, but
other use both forms in either sense.   /-y/ is ⫽-e⫽ after lax
vowels and /-i/ after tense vowels, e.g., ⫽mebae⫽, 'I come', and
⫽mebaeɛ⫽, 'when I came'.   (3) See Unit 18, note 5 for past tense
secondary tones.
    With verbs stems ending in nasals and semivowels, some (es-
pecially younger) speakers have a long nasal or semivowel in the
intransitive just as in the transitive, but many speakers have
/-ey/ and /-eyɛ/ with this type of stem, e.g., /mɛ̃tónèy/, 'I
bought it (or some), /mɛ̃tónèyɛ/, 'when I bought it (or some)'.
These endings are ⫽-ee⫽ and /-eeɛ⫽.
    It is often necessary to supply <u>impersonal</u> pronoun objects
in English when translating Twi intransitive verbs, such as, 'it',
'one', 'some', 'any', or 'none', e.g., /mɛ̃tóòy/, 'I bought it',
or 'I bought some'.

2.   The affirmative perfect tense is marked by a low-tone /a- ˜
a̧-/ prefix to the first verb of a subject plus high tone on the
first syllable of the verb.   Succeeding syllables of the verb

are all high except the last which is low. But in the second
person, a contracted form usually occurs, e.g., /wúàkódìdí/ is
replaced by /wákòdìdí/ and is //woakodidi//. Contracted forms occur
in other persons, but there is no tone change in the first and
third persons. In the orthography, the uncontracted form is used
except in the first person singular.

makó //mako//	I have gone	yakó //yɛako//	we have gone
wákò //woako//	you have gone	mákò //moako//	you have gone
wakó //wako//	he, she, it has gone	wakó //woako// (Compare note 15)	they have gone
akó //ako//	it has gone	akó //ako//	they have gone

3.   The past negative is the perfect affirmative plus a low-tone
nasal before the stem, e.g., /mínnidììyɛ/, which is //minnidiiɛ//.
means 'I haven't eaten' and NOT 'I didn't eat.'

The perfect negative is the past affirmative plus a low-tone
nasal before the stem, e.g., /maŋkó/ means I didn't go', and NOT
'I haven't gone'. The perfect negative has all the transitive
and intransitive forms parallel to those of the past affirmative.
See note 1.

4.   The subjunctive affirmative is marked by a low-tone homorganic nasal prefix plus a high tone on the first syllable of the
verb. Succeeding syllables have their simple-stem tones, e.g.,
/yɛŋkódìdí/, 'we should go eat'.

Pattern Drill A

1. M(ɑ̃) yɛŋkó.   Let's go.
2. M(ɑ̃) yɛnnídì.   Let's eat.
3. M(ɑ̃) yɛŋkó fíe.   Let's go home.
4. M(ɑ̃) yɛŋkó áfèì.   Let's go now.
5. M(ɑ̃) yɛññyìna.   Let's stop.
6. M(ɑ̃) °yɛntɛ́rɑ̃ ɑ̃sɛ.   Let's sit down.

Pattern Drill B

1. Mɑ̃ nõ ŋkó.   Let him go.   Have him go.
2. Mɑ̃ wɔn ŋkó.   Let them go.   Have them go.
3. Mɑ̃ ɔbarɛ́mà nõ ŋkó.   Let the man go.

4. Mɛ̃́ <u>obáa nɔ̃́ ŋkó</u>.   Let the woman go.

5. Mɛ̃́ <u>abɔfára nɔ̃́ ŋkó</u>.   Let the child go.

6. Mɛ̃́ <u>akwadaá nɔ̃́ ŋkó</u>.   Let the infant go.

Pattern Drill C

1. °Ɛmmɛ̃́ <u>yéŋkó</u>.   Let's not go.

2. Ɛmmɛ̃́ <u>yénnıdí</u>.   Let's not eat.

3. Ɛmmɛ̃́ <u>yéŋkó fíe</u>.   Let's not go home.

4. Ɛmmɛ̃́ <u>yéŋkó ɛ́fèı</u>.   Let's not go now.

5. Ɛmmɛ̃́ <u>yénnyıná</u>.   Let's not stop.

6. Ɛmmɛ̃́ <u>yéntɛrɛ̃́ ɛ̃́sɛ̨</u>.   Let's not sit down.

Pattern Drill D

1. Ɛmmɛ̃́ <u>nɔ̃́ ŋkó</u>.   Don't let him go.

2. Ɛmmɛ̃́ <u>wɔŋ ŋkó</u>.   Don't let them go.

3. Ɛmmɛ̃́ <u>ɔbarɛ̨má nɔ̃́ ŋkó</u>.   Don't let the man go.

4. Ɛmmɛ̃́ <u>ɔbáa nɔ̃́ ŋkó</u>.   Don't let the woman go.

5. Ɛmmɛ̃́ <u>abɔfára nɔ̃́ ŋkó</u>.   Don't let the child go.

6. Ɛmmɛ̃́ <u>akwadaá nɔ̃́ ŋkó</u>.   Don't let the infant go.

New words

       gyına   to stop, stand, rest, come to a
                               standing or upright position

     °tɛrɛ̃́, tɛnɛ̃́   to sit, live, stay

Pattern Drill E

1. Mɛ̃kɔɔ Ŋkɛɾã́ñ nnéra.   I went to Accra yesterday.

2. Ɔbaa há nnéra.   He came here yesterday.

3. Mĩ́hũu nṍ nnéra.   I saw him yesterday.

4. Yɛtɔɔ mpabɔá nnéra.   We bought some shoes yesterday.

5. Mṍhwɛ̀hwɛ́ɛ̀ nṍ nnéra.   You (pl.) looked for him
                               yesterday.

6. Wɔ́tɔnɩ̀ ŋkɔ́kɔ́ nnéra.   You sold some chickens
                               yesterday.

7. Womã̃a mĩ́ sɪká nṍ nnéra.   They gave me the money
                               yesterday.

8. Mɛ̃dɛ bɪrɪbí bɛɾɛ̀ɛ̀ wɔ   I brought you something
   nnéra.   yesterday.

9. Mɛ̃dɛ nṍ baa nnéra.   I brought him yesterday.

10. Mɛ̃dɛ nṍ kɔɔ nnéra.   I sent him away yesterday.

Pattern Drill F

1. Maŋkó Ŋkɛɾã́ñ nnéra.   I didn't go to Accra yesterday.

2. Wammá há nnéra.   He didn't come here yesterday.

3. Mã́ŋhṹ nṍ nnéra.   I didn't see him yesterday.

4. °Yantó mpabɔá nnéra.   We didn't buy any shoes
                               yesterday.

5. °Maŋhwɛhwɛ́ nṍ nnéra.   You (pl.) didn't look for him
                               yesterday.

6. °Wàntóñ ŋkɔ́kɔ́ nnéra.   You didn't sell any chickens
                               yesterday.

83

7. <u>ᵉWammá mí sıká nó</u>   They dıdn't gıve me the money
   nnéra.   yesterday.

8. <u>Mamfá bırıbí ámmęrɛ wǫ</u>   I dıdn't brıng you anythıng
   nnéra.   yesterday.

9. <u>Mamfá nó ámma</u> nnɛrá.   I dıdn't brıng hım yesterday.

10. <u>Mamfá nó áŋkɔ</u> nnéra.   I dıdn't send hım away
                                    yesterday.

New words

    akǫ́kɔ́ (pl. ŋ-)   chıcken

    dę   to have, own; cause, make,
                                    force

    bęrɛ́   to brıng somethıng to a
                                    person

    dę...ba   to brıng a person

    dę...kɔ   to send away, cause to go

Pattern Drıll G

1. <u>Makɔ́ sǫ́tɔɔ́ mú dedąw.</u>   I have already gone to the
                                    store.

2. <u>Mąkóhũ dókęta dedąw.</u>   I've already gone to see the
                                    doctor.

3. <u>Mądí ąnopą́ądùąnę́ dedąw.</u>   I've already eaten breakfast.

4. <u>Wądí ewĩ́mũ̃ądùąnę́ dedąw.</u>   He has already eaten lunch.

5. <u>Wadí añw̃ummér̃eadùané</u>   They have already eaten dınner.
   dedąw.

6. Wanõà nám nṍ dedąw.   They have already cooked the
                                         meat.

7. Wabá dedąw.   They have already come.

8. Yakósęrà ɔkyɛrɛkyérɛnì   We have already gone to
   nṍ dedąw.   visit the teacher.

9. Wákyęrè nṍ ákyęréẅ   You have already taught him
   dedąw.   to write.

10. Mákyęrè mí ofíe nṍ dedąw.   You have already shown me
                                         the house.

Pattern Drill H

1. Mẽ̀ŋkóɔ̀ sɔ́tɔɔ̀ mṹ ɛɛ.   I haven't gone to the store
                                         yet.

2. Mẽ̀ŋkóhũù dókę̀ta ɛɛ.   I haven't gone to see the
                                         doctor yet.

3. Mĩ̀mìí ąnɔpáą̀dùąnó ɛɛ.   I haven't eaten breakfast yet.

4. Onnìì eẅímũadùąné ɛɛ.   He hasn't eaten lunch yet.

5. Wonnìì ą̀ẅumméreądùąné ɛɛ.   They haven't eaten dinner yet.

6. Wɔnnõ̀áà nám nṍ ɛɛ.   They haven't cooked the
                                         meat yet.

7. Wɔɔmáàyɛ.   They haven't come yet.

8. Yɛŋkósęraà ɔkyɛrɛkyérɛnì   We haven't gone to visit
   nṍ ɛɛ.   the teacher yet.

85

9. <u>Wǫ́ŋ̀kyę́réɛ̀ nǒ akyę́réw̌</u>   You haven't taught him to

     ɛ ɛ.   read yet.

10. <u>Mǒ́ŋ̀kyę́réɛ̀ mɛ̌ ofíe nǒ</u>   You haven't shown me the

     ɛ ɛ.   house yet.

New words

     anɔpą́ą̀dùą̀nę́   breakfast

     ew̌ıą́, ąw̌ıą́   sunshine; noon, late forenoon, and early afternoon

     ew̌ıą́ą̀dùą̀nę   lunch, noon meal

     ąñw̌ummę́reą̀dùą̀nę́   supper, evening meal

7. /tę̀rǎ́/ ıs // tra//.

8. The third person imperative, ı.e., the form meaning 'to have someone have someone else do something' ıs marked by the causative /mǎ/ at the beginning of the sentence and a low-tone nasal prefix on the verb plus a high tone on the last syllable of the verb, e.g., /mǎ nǒ ŋkó/, 'Have him go', or 'Let him go'.

9. The negative cohortative ıs marked by the negative of /mǎ/ plus a high tone on /yɛ́/, a low tone on the nasal prefix, and a high tone on the last syllable of the verb, e.g., /ɛmmǎ yɛ̀ŋkó/, 'Let's not go'. /ɛmmǎ/ ıs sometimes /mmǎ/ and ıs // mma//.

10. /ñgyıná/ ıs /ññyıná/. Compare Unıt 3, note 12.

11. Note CAREFULLY that the past negative looks like a perfect positive plus a negative prefix and that the perfect negative looks like a·past positive plus a negative prefix.

12. The perfect negative has a low tone on the last syllable and a high on the next to last. Other syllables are the same tone as ın the present.

13. /dẹ/ has a suppletive negative /mfá/, which is the negative
of /fa/, 'take'. The verb after /mfá/ is in the consecutive form,
e.g., /Mamfá biribi ámmɛrɛ wọ nnéra/, 'I didn't bring you anything
yesterday', 'I didn't take anything to bring to you yesterday'.

14. Vowel harmony does not usually influence more than one vowel
across word boundaries or across stem boundaries in a nominal
compound where there is more than one stem. For example, the
usual form is /anɔpáạdùạné/; one will seldom hear /ạnopáạdùạné/.

15. In fast speech it is often impossible to tell the third
person plural perfect from the third person singular because the
(ɔ- ~ o-) of the plural pronoun may be elided; /woạdí/ alternates
with /wạdí/, 'they have eaten'. If context does not indicate
clearly whether the subject is plural or singular, /wón nɔ́/ is
used, e.g., /wón nɔ́ ạdí/.

16. /ạñwummedùạné/, 'supper' also occurs.

/eẅiạ́ mú ạduạné/, 'lunch', 'noon meal' is also common.

17. The Twi dictionary still uses the symbol 'ŋ'; consequently,
words like /ạñwummérẹ/, 'evening', and /ngɔ́/, 'oil', will have to
be looked up under //ɔ//. In the dictionary //ɔ// follows /n//. The
revised orthography no longer uses this symbol. The glossary at
the end of this manual does not use 'ŋ'.

18. /fa/, 'to take' occurs with both a high and a low stem
vowel in the simple present, i.e., some speakers say /mɛ́fa/,
others /mɛ̃fá/.

Unit 10

Basic Dialogue

-A-

1	Mɛ̃kɔɔ Ŋkɛrɑ̃n nnéra.	I went to Accra yesterday.

-B-

2	Wɔ́kɔ̀yɛ̀ɛ̀ dɛ̌ɛ̃̀?	What did you go to do?

-A-

	ntãmã́	clothes, Ghanian dress
3	Mɛ̃tɔɔ ntãmã́.	I bought some clothes.

-B-

	ńsɔsɔ	also, else
4	ɛdɛ́ɛ bɛ̃́n ńsɔsɔ na wɔ́yɛɛ́?	What else did you do?

-A-

5	Mɛ̃kɔɔyɛ sɛ́ɛ́ mĩ̀kohṹ ɔyarɛsáfɔ́ɔ.	I went especially to see the doctor.
	sɛ̨	to say
6	Ɔyarɛsáfɔ́ɔ nɔ̃́ sɛ̨́ mɛ̃́nkɔda.	The doctor said I should go to bed.
7	ɛdɛ̨ɛ̃́n ntí na ᵒwɔ̨́nkɔ̀daayɛ?	Why haven't you gone to bed?
	séèseì	until now, as yet, still
8	Mĩ̀kó fíe séèseì.	I'm on my way home now.

88

Notes

1. Verbs of motion have objects. In the sentence /Mɛ̃kɔɔ Ŋkɛrã̃ñ/, 'I went to Accra', /Ŋkɛrã̃ñ/ is the object of the verb /kɔ/.

2. /kɔ/ plus the consecutive form is one way of expressing purpose, e.g., /mɛ̃kɔɔ áhũ nõ/, 'I want to see him'. To express emphatic purpose /sɛ́ɛ̀/ plus another /kɔ/ with a subject is used, e.g., /Mɛ̃kɔɔyɛ sɛ́ɛ̀ mɪ̃kohũ nõ/, 'I went purposely to see him'. Note that the first /kɔ/ is intransitive and adverbial. See note 5.

The consecutive form does not occur after the habitual present, but /mɛ̃kɔɔ kohũ̃ũ nõ/, 'I go to see him (regularly)'.

3. When /sɛ̨/, 'to say', is used to quote or relate instructions, it is followed by the subjunctive, e.g., /Ɔsɛ̨́ mɛ̃nkó/, 'He said I should go', /Ɔsɛ̨́ mɛ̃ǹkó/, 'He said I shouldn't go'.

4. /sɛ́ɛsei/ indicates that the verb refers to a particular time segment. With the present or simple verb, it means 'right now', or 'in the act of', e.g., /Mɪ̃kó fie sɛ́ɛsiè/, 'I am in the act of going home right now'.

Grammatical Drill A

Change to past positive.

1.	Yɛkó.	Yɛkɔɔy.
2.	Ohṹ.	Ohũ̃uy.
3.	Mɪ̃dɪdí.	Mɪ̃dɪdíiy.
4.	Wóyɛ.	Wóyɛɛ̀.
5.	Wotɔ́ṇ.	Wotonẹẹ.
6.	Mũbɪsá.	Mũbɪsáay.
7.	Ɔbá.	Ɔbaay.
8.	Mɛ̃hwɛ́.	Mɛ̃hwɛɛ.
9.	Mɛ̃tó.	Mɛ̃tɔɔy.

89

10. Wɔnɔ́á.   Wɔnɔ́aày.

11. Yɛfá   Yɛfaay.

12. Ɔyɛ̗ɾéw.   Ɔkyɛ̗ɾéwɛ̗̀.

13. Wɔ̗dà.   Wɔ̗daày.

14. Wokɛ́.   Wokɛ́ay.

15. Osṹɑ̗́.   Osṹɑ̗́aày.

16. Mɛ̃nɔ̃́m.   Mɛ̃nɔ̃́mɛ̗ɛ̗.

17. Wokohṹ.   Wokohṹ̀uy.

18. Mɔ́gyɛ̗̀.   Mɔ́gyɛ̗ɛ̗̀.

19. Ɔfɛ̗ɾɛ́.   Ɔfɛ̗ɾɛ́ɛ̀.

20. Ɔmɛ́.   Ɔmɛ̃́ay.

Grammatical Drill B

Change to past positive.

1. Mɛ̃sɛ̗ɾá mɛ́ papá.   I visit my father.

    Mɛ̃sɛ̗ɾáà mɛ́ papá.   I visited my father.

2. Ohṹ mɛ̃́.   He sees me.

    Ohṹu mɛ̃́.   He saw me.

3. Ɔbá behṹ mɛ̃́.   He comes to see me.

    Ɔbaa behṹ̀u mɛ̃́.   He came to see me.

4. Ɔbá sɛ́ɛ̀ obehṹ mɛ̃́.   He comes purposely to see me.

    Ɔbaayɛ sɛ́ɛ̀ obehṹ mɛ̃́.   He came purposely to see me.

5. Mɛ̃tɔ́ǹ ntɛ̃́mɛ́.   I sell clothes.

    Mɛ̃tɔ́ɲ̀ ntɛ̃́mɛ́.   I sold clothes.

6. Mĩ́bisa nɔ̃́.   I ask him.

    Mĩ́bisáà nɔ̃́.   I asked him.

90

7. Ɔtó ɑ̨kutú.   He buys oranges.

   Ɔtɔɔ ɑ̨kutú.   He bought oranges.

8. Mɛ̃dɛ̨ ɑ̨kutú bɛ̨rɛ́ nő.   I bring him an orange.

   Mɛ̨dɛ̨ ɑ̨kutú bɛ̨rɛ́ɛ̀ nő.   I brought him an orange.

9. Wúbùé ɲhőmã̃ nő.   You open the book.

   Wúbùéè ɲhőmã̃ nő.   You opened the book.

10. Ɔbá ᵒbɛgyɛ́ ɲhőmã̃.   He comes to get the book.

    Ɔbaayɛ bɛgyɛ́ɛ̨̀ ɲhőmã̃.   He came to get the book.

Lexical Drill A

1. Mɛ̃kɔɔ Ŋkɛ̨rã̃n nnɛ́ra.   I went to Accra yesterday.

2. Mɛ̃tɔɔ ká̀à fɔ́fɔ́rɔ̨ wɔ   I bought a new car at Accra
   Nkɛ̨rã̃n nnɛ́ra.   yesterday.

3. Mɛ̃tɔɔ ká̀à fɔ́fɔ́rɔ̨ mã̃a   I bought a new car for my
   mɛ̃ yɛ̨rɛ̨.   wife.

4. Matɔ́ ká̀à fɔ́fɔ́rɔ̨ ámã̃ mɛ̃   I have bought another car for
   yɛ̨rɛ̨.   my wife.

5. Matɔ́ ká̀à mɑ̨fìrɪ nɛ́   I have bought a car from him.
   fɪkyɛ́ñ.

6. Watɔ́ ká̀à ɑ̨fɪrɪ nɛ́   She has bought a car from him.
   fɪkyɛ́ñ.

7. Wabá sɛ́ɛ̀ ɔbɛtɔ́ ká̀à   She has come purposely to buy
   ɑ̨fɪrɪ nɛ́ fɪkyɛ́ñ.   a car from him.

8. Wabá sɛ́ɛ̀ ɔbɛtɔ́ ntamá̃   She has come especially to buy
   ámã̃ nɛ̃ bá.   clothes for her child.

91

9. °Éèbía̧ ɔbétɔ ntāmā́ ámā̀   She may buy clothes for her
   nɛ̃ bá.   child.

10. Éèbía̧ ɔbétɔ ak̄ōññūá̧   Maybe she will buy some chairs
    fíe.   for the house.

New words

    fófórɔ   new, another

    ñkyɛ́ñ   side; from, apart, by, near

    éèbía̧   perhaps, maybe

Lexical Drill B

1. Mɛ̄tóŋ mɛ̃ kóòkoò mā̄ nɔ̃.   I sell my cocoa to him.

2. Mɛ̄etóŋ mɛ̃ kóòkoò ā́mā̀ nɔ̃.   I'm selling my cocoa to him.

3. Mɛ̄etóŋ mɪ̄ fíe áà ɛwɔ   I'm selling my house at Accra.
   Ŋkɛrā́n nɔ̃́.

4. Mɛ̄ekɔsɛ́raà mɪ́ nūa̧ nɔ̃́ áà   I visited my brother who is at
   ɔwɔ Ŋkɛrā́n nɔ̃́.   Accra.

5. Mɛ̄ekɔsɛ́raà mɪ́ nūa̧ nɔ̃́   I visited my brother when I
   mmɛ́r(ę) áà ná mɛ̃wɔ   was in Accra.
   Ŋkɛrā́n.

6. Mɪ̄kohū̀ù dókę̀ta nɔ̃́ mmɛ́r(ę) I went to see the doctor when
   áà ná mɛ̃wɔ Ŋkɛrā́n nɔ̃́.   I was in Accra.

7. Mɪ̄kohū̀ù dókę̀ta nɔ̃́   I went to see the doctor
   és(ɪ)a̧nę sɛ́ɛ́ ná   because I was sick.
   mɛ̄yarę́.

8. M̃tệráà fíe ésiàne sɛ́ɛ̀   I stayed home because I was
   ná m̃yarệ.   sick.

9. M̃tệráà fíe kosí sɛ́ɛ̀   I stayed home until he came.
   ɔbaayɛ.

10. M̃twɛṇṇ kosí sɛ́ɛ̀ ɔbaayɛ. I waited until he came.

New words

    kookóò, (kóókoò)   cocoa
    abẹ́rẹ (pl. m-)   time
    mmẹ́rẹ áà   when, (time that)
    ésiǎnẹ   because, on account of
    kosí   until, up to
    twɛṇ   to wait

Lexical Drill C

1. Ɔkó sɔ́tɔò mú.   He is gone to the store.

2. Wabá firi sɔ́tɔò mú.   He has come back from the
                              store.

3. Wabá firi Koforíduạ.   He has come back from
                              Koforidua.

4. Masáň ábà Koforíduạ.   I have returned to Koforidua.

5. Masáň ábà rẹbɛgyẹ́ mé   I have returned to get my
   hómã nố.   book.

6. Kofí rẹbɛgyẹ mé hómã   Kofi has come to get my book.
   nố.

7. Kofí áhwɛ̀hwɛ́ wǫ dá mú   Kofı has been looking for you
   yí ñyɪ̃ááã.   all day.

8. Ámma áhwɛ̀hwɛ́ wǫ dá mú   Amma has been looking for you
   yí ñyɪ̃ááã.   all day.

9. Ámma súáā̧ Bǫrɔfǫkáā wɔ   Amma studied English ın Ghana.
   Ghana.

10. Ɛdǫ́ɛ̃n ntí na wúsúáā̧   Why dıd you study Englısh ın
    Bǫrɔfǫkáā wɔ Ghánà.   Ghana?

Lexıcal Drıll D

1. Ɔyarǫsáfǫ̀ɔ nɔ́ sǫ́   The doctor saıd I should go to
   mɛ́ŋkɔda.   bed.

2. Ɔyarǫsáfǫ̀ɔ nɔ́ sǫ́   The doctor saıd ıt ıs necessary
   ɛsɛ sɛ́ɛ̀ ɔfá ǫ̧dùru yí.   for hım to take thıs medıcıne.

3. Ɔyarǫhwɛ́fǫ̀ɔ nɔ́ sǫ́   The nurse saıd he has to
   ɛsɛ sɛ́ɛ̀ ɔfá ǫ̧dùru yí.   take thıs medıcıne.

4. Ɔyarǫhwɛ́fǫ̀ɔ nɔ́ sǫ́   The doctor saıd he should take
   ómfa ǫ̧dùru yí.   thıs medıcıne.

5. Nɛ̃ bǫ̀àfǫ̀ɔ nɔ́ sǫ́ ómfa   His assistant saıd he should
   ǫ̧dùru yí.   take the medıcıne.

6. Nɛ̃ bǫ̀àfǫ̀ɔ nɔ́ baa behúũ   His assistant came to see hım.
   nɔ̃́.

7. Akyǫrɛkyǫ́rɛ̀fǫ̀ɔ nɔ́ baa   The teachers came to see hım.
   behúũ nɔ̃́.

8. Akyǫrɛkyǫ́rɛ̀fǫ̀ɔ nɔ́ baayɛ   The teachers were here pur-
   sɛ́ɛ̀ wobehúũ nɔ̃́.   posely to see hım.

9. Mɛ́ papá baayɛ séɛ́   My father came especially to
    obehǔ nɔ̌.   see him.

10. Mɛ́ papá firi Amɛ́rèka   My father is back from America
     ábà, na ɔwɔ Kumásę.   and he is at Kumasi.

11. Mɪ́ nǔ̟ḁbarɛmá nɔ̌ firi   My brother is back from America
     Amɛ́rèka ábà na ɔwɔ   and he is at Kumasi.
     Kumásę.

12. Mɪ́ nǔ̟ḁbarɛmá nɔ̌ firi   My brother has already come
     Amɛ́rèka ábà, na ɔwɔ   back from America and he is
     Kumásę séisei.   (living) at Kumasi now.

5. /bɛ- ~ be-/, 'come in order to', 'come for', is used to form
compound verbs, e.g., /mɛ̌bɛgyę́/, 'I come to get'. /bɛ-/ express‑
ing purpose has a low tone unless preceded by a perfect prefix
/a-/, then it has high tone. /bɛ́-/ indicating future is always
high and is followed by a high.

    /ba/, 'come' may precede a compund verb beginning with the
/bɛ-/ of purpose, e.g., /Ɔbá behǔ mɛ̌/, 'He comes to see me'. If
/séɛ́/ occurs between /ba/ and /bɛ-/, the verb with /bɛ-/ also has
a subject and the meaning is emphatic, e.g., /Ɔbaayɛ séɛ́ obehǔ mɛ̌/,
'He comes purposely or especially to see me'. Compare note 2.

    /bɛ- ~ be-/ also is used to express ingressive aspect, i.e.,
'about to', e.g., /mɪ́ibedídɪ/, 'I am about to eat'. Ingressive
/bɛ- ~ be-/ occurs only with the progressive form of the verb.
/bɛ- ~ be-/ expressing purpose occurs with the habitual or simple
form of the verb.

    /bɛ-/ is usually //be//, e.g., /mɛ̌bɛgyę́/ is //mebegye//.

6.   /kɔ/ also means, 'to go with', 'match', 'suit', as /Éèbíą̀
ɔbétɔ akoñguą́ ákɔ̀ fíe/, 'Maybe she will buy some chairs to go with
the house', i.e., chairs which will go well with the furnishings
already in the house.

7.   In a sentence like that in Lexical Drill A, sentence 5, where
there is an object after the first verb, the consecutive form has
a high tone prefix and may also have a <u>first person singular</u> pronoun prefix. See also Unit 5, note 4.

8.   /éèbíą̀/ is //ɛ́bıa//. //éèbíą̀//, 'perhaps', 'maybe', also corresponds to English 'may', e.g., /éèbíà ɔbétɔ/, translates 'Maybe she
will buy' or 'She may buy'.

9.   Stative verbs, i.e., verbs which refer to a state or condition, are usually not inflected for tense. A number of suppletive
forms or periphrastic constructions are employed. Compare Unit 5,
note 13.

     Past time may be indicated in a stative verb by putting /ná/
at the beginning of the sentence or immediately after the conjunction if the stative verb occurs with other than the first grammatical subject of the sentence. If past time is clear from context
/ná/ does not always occur. See Lexical Drill B, sentences 5, 6,
7, and 8 for examples of the stative verbs /wɔ/ and /yarę/. See
also Unit 11, note 10.

     /ná/ is also used with the progressive aspect to indicate <u>both</u>
past and future. Context has to tell whether /ná mẽekɔtɔ́/ is 'I
was going to buy' or 'I will be going to buy'.

     /ná/ occur at the <u>beginning</u> of a sentence before any simple
present verb and means 'used to'.

10. /Amę́rèka/ is //Amerıka//.

Unit 11

Basic Dialogue

-A-

wǫ	to beget, give birth to
1 Ɛhɛ́fá na yɛwǫ́ǫ̀ wǫ?	Where were you born?

-B-

2 Yɛwǫ́ǫ̀ mẽ wo Kumásę.	I was born at Kumase.

-A-

afǫ́ (pl. mfíe)	year
ahɛ́	how many, how much
3 Mfíe áhɛ̀ na wǫ̀dɪ?	How old are you? ('Years how many then you have used up? ')

-B-

ąduasɛ́	thirty
4 Mądí mfíe ąduąsɛ́.	I'm thirty years old.

-A-

ądwúma (ǫ̀dwùma) (pl. ññw̌úma)	work, occupation
5 Ɛdęɛ̌ñ ą́dwùma na wó̦yɛ?	What's your occupation? ('What kind work then you do? ')

-B-

abɛ́ñ (ábɛ́ñ) (pl. m-)	a large or strong building, the government
6 Mẽyɛ́ ábɛ́ñ ą́dwùma.	I work for the government.

-A-

tɛ̇	to live, dwell
7 Ɛhéfá na wɔ́tɛ̀?	Where do you live?

-B-

8 Mɐtɛ̇ Tamalɛ̇.	I live at Tamale.

Grammatical Drill A

Change to perfect positive.

1.	Yɛkó.	Yakó.
2.	Ohů.	Wą̊hů.
3.	Mídidí.	Mą̊dídɪ.
4.	Wɔ́yɛ.	Wáyɛ̀.
5.	Wotóŋ.	watóŋ
6.	Mǔbìsá.	Mą̊bìsá.
7.	Ɔba.	Wabá.
8.	Mɐ̃hwɛ́.	Mahwɛ́.
9.	Mɐtó.	Mató.
10.	Wonóá.	Wanóa
11.	Yɛfá.	Yafá.
12.	Ɔkyɛ́rɛ́w.	Wakyɛ́rɛ̀w.
13.	Wɔ́dà.	Wáda.
14.	Wokå̃.	Wakå̃
15.	Osů̃ą́.	Wą̊sů̃ą́.
16.	Mɐ̃nóm.	Manóm.
17.	Wúkòhů̃	Wą́kòhů̃

18. Mɔ́gyę.   Mágyę̀

19. Ɔfęré.   Wafę́rɛ.

20. Ɔmɑ̃́.   Wamɑ̃́.

Question and Answer Drill A

1. Dá bɛ́n na wowǫǫ wǫ?   What day were you born?

   Wowǫǫ mɛ̃ Efíeda.   I was born on Friday.

2. Ɛhɛ́fɑ́ na wǫ́tę ɑ̨́fèɪ?   Where are you living now?

   Mɛ̃tę Tamalę ɑ̨́fèɪ.   I'm living at Tamale now.

3. Ɛdęɛ́n ntí wǫ́ko kohũu   Why did you go see the doctor?
   dókęta?

   Mɛ̃kó kohũu dókęta   I went to see the doctor

   esíɑ̨̀nę̀ sɛ́ɛ̀ nɑ́   because I was sick.

   mɑ̃́yaré.

4. Ɛdęɛ́n ntí wǫ́sɑ̃́ń báayè?   Why did you come back?

   Mɛ̃sɑ̃́ń báayè sɛ́ɛ̀   I came back to see you.

   míɪbehṹ wǫ.

5. Ɛhɛ́fɑ́ na yɛwǫ́ǫ́ wǫ?   Where were you born?

   Yɛwǫǫ mɛ̃ wo Kumásę   I was born at Kumase

   ayaręsábę̀a.   hospital.

6. Ɛhɛ́fɑ́ na yɛwǫǫ nó?   Where was he born?

   Yɛwǫ́ǫ́ nó wo   He was born at the hospital

   ayaręsábę̀a áà ɛwo   in Kumase.

   Kumásę.

7. Mfíe áhɛ̃ na wọ bá ạdí?   How old is your child?

    Mɛ̃ bá ạdí <u>afẹ́</u>.   My child is a year old.

8. Ɛhɛ́fá na wọ́yɛ ạdwùma?   Where do you work?

    Mɛ̃yɛ́ ạdwùma <u>wọ</u>   I work at Takoradi.

    <u>Tạ̀kòrạdí</u>.

9. Wọ́yɛɛ̀ ạdwúma mɛ̃anɔ̃?   Did you use to work for him?

    <u>Ạ́ạ̃ñ</u>, mɛ̃yɛɛ̀ ạdwúma mɛ̃a   Yes, I used to work for him.

    nɔ̃.

10. Mfíe ahɛ́ wạ̀dì wọ há?   How long have you been here?

    <u>Mạdí afẹ́</u> wọ há.   I have been here a year.

Lexical Drill A

1. Ná mɛ̃ nɛ́ñ yɛ mɛ̃ yá   My leg hurt yesterday.

    nnɛra.

2. <u>Opiráà nɛ̃ nɛ́ñ</u> nnɛra.   He hurt his leg yesterday.

3. Opiráà nɛ̃ nɛ́ñ <u>ansɛ́ na</u>   He hurt his leg before I

    <u>mĩ̀bedú hó</u>.   arrived.

4. <u>Ná ọwɔ hó</u> ansɛ́ na   He was there before I arrived.

    mĩ̀bedú hó.

5. <u>Mĩnĩm sɛ́ɛ̀</u> ná ọwɔ hó.   I know that he was there.

6. Mĩnĩm sɛ́ɛ̀ <u>ọwɔ hó</u>.   I know he is there.

7. Ɔsẹ́ ọwɔ hó.   He said he was there.

8. Ɔsé <u>wọwɔ hó</u>.   He said they were there.

9. <u>Ná mĩnĩm</u> sɛ́ɛ̀ wọwɔ hó.   I know they were there.

10. Ná mĩnĩm sɛ́ɛ̀ <u>ọwɔ hó</u>.   I know he was there.

New words

pırá	to ınjure, be ınjured
ansá	fırst, at fırst, meanwhıle
ansá na	before (ın tıme)
du, duru	to descend, arrıve

Pattern Drıll A

1. Mądídı ą̌wìe.   I have fınıshed eatıng.
2. Makéŋkáñ ą̌wìe.   I have fınıshed readıng.
3. Makyę́rɛw ą̌wìe.   I have fınıshed wrıtıng.
4. Mayɛ́ ą́dwùma áwìe.   I have fınıshed workıng.
5. Masúą ádę̀ ą̌wìe.   I have fınıshed studyıng.

Pattern Drıll B

1. Mą̌wíò yɑ̌ɪ̀ɪ̀ɪ́.   I have fınıshed eatıng
2. Mą̌wíè akéŋkáñ.   I have fınıshed readıng.
3. Mą̌wíè akyę́rɛ́w.   I have fınıshed wrıtıng.
4. Mą̌wíè ą́dwúmayɛ.   I have fınıshed workıng.
5. Mą̌wíè ą́desúą́.   I have fınıshed studyıng.

Pattern Drıll C

1. Ɔsę́ mę́mmara.   He saıd I should come.
2. Ɔsę́ mę̃mmá.   He saıd I shouldn't come.
3. Ɔsę́ mę́nto bí.   He saıd I should buy some.
4. Ɔsę́ mę̃nntó bí.   He saıd I shouldn't buy any.
5. Ɔsę́ mę́ŋko fíe.   He saıd I should go home.

6. Ɔsɛ́ <u>mɛnkó fíe</u>.   He said I shouldn't go home.

7. Ɔsɛ́ <u>mɛ́nsũã</u>.   He said I should learn it.

8. Ɔsɛ́ <u>mɛ̃nsũã́</u>.   He said I shouldn't learn it.

9. Ɔsɛ́ <u>mɛ́ŋkɔda</u>.   He said I should go to bed.

10. Ɔsɛ́ <u>mɛ̃ŋkɔdá</u>.   He said I should not go to bed.

Question and Answer Drill B

1. Bɛ́rɛ ɑ̨́dù?   Is it time?

     <u>Dɑ̨ɑ̨bí</u>, bɛ́rɛ nnúùyɛ.   No, it isn't time yet.

2. Ná wɔ̨́yɛ̀ sukúùní wɔ   Were you a student in Ghana?

     Ghánà?

     <u>Dɑ̨ɑ̨bí</u>, ná mɛ̃ñyɛ́   No, I wasn't a student in

     sukúùní wɔ Ghánà.   Ghana.

3. Mfíe ahɛ̃́ na wátɛ̨nã́ há?   How long have you lived here?

     Matɛ̨nã́ há <u>fírɪ</u>   I have lived here since I

     <u>mmɛ̨́r(ɛ) ɑ̨́à yɛwɔ̨ɔ̨ mɛ̃́</u>.   was born.

4. Ɛhɛ̃́ na ná wɔ̨́wɔ̀ Ghánà?   Where were you in Ghana?

     Ná mɛ̃wɔ <u>Nsawam</u>.   I was at Nsawam.

5. Mmɛ̨́rɛ bɛ̃́n na ná wɔ̨́wɔ̀   When were you in Kumasi?

     Kumásɛ̨?

     Ná mɛ̃wɔ Kumásɛ̨   I was in Kumasi Sunday.

     <u>Kwɑ̨sièda</u>.

6. Ɛhɛ̃́ na wɔtɛ̨?   Where do they live?

     Ɛhá <u>na</u> wɔtɛ̨.   Here /is where/ they live.

7. Wɑ̨́wìè ɑ̨́dwúmayɛ?   Have you finished working?

     <u>Mɪ́bewíé</u> ɑ̨́dwùmayɛ́.   I am about to finish working.

8. Ɛhéfá na ɔtɛ ɑ̀fèɪ?   Where does he live now?

   Fíe yí mú na ɔtɛ ɑ̀fèɪ.   This is the house where he

                                   lives now.

9. Héna na ɑ̀búe báɛ̀gɛ nó́ɤ   Who has opened the bag?

   Mĩnnĩm nɛa obúeè báɛ̀gɛ   I don't know who opened the

   nó́.   bag.

10. Mmɛ́rɛ bɛ́n na ɔteráà há?   When did he live here?

    Ɔtɛráà há nɛ́   He lived here during his

    mmɔfáraasɛ̀.   childhood.

New words

    ɛhéna (pl. -nõm)   who, whom, whose

    báɛ̀gɛ   bag, sack, briefcase

    mmɔfáraasɛ̀   childhood

Notes

1. One of the names which every Akan child receives corresponds
to the name of the day of the week he was born on.

	Day	Male	Female
Sunday	Kwɑsíeda	Kwɑsí	Ʌkósuɑ
Monday	Dwɔ́ɔda	Kwadwɔ́	Adwɔ́à
Tuesday	Bɛnada	Kwabɛná	Ábɛnaa
Wednesday	Wúkuoda	Kwɑkú	Ʌkúɑ̀
Thursday	Yáwòda	Yaw	Yaá
Friday	Fíeda	Kofí	Afúɑ̀
Saturday	Mɛ́mɛ̀nɛda	Kwámɛ̀	Ámma

103

2. The third person plural is also sometimes used with a passive meaning, e.g., /wɔwɔɔ mɛ̃/, 'I was born', literally, 'they bore me'. Compare Unit 5, note 8 and Unit 7, note 14.

3. /Ɔwɔ ayarɛsábɛ̀a áà ɛwɔ Ŋkɛ̀rã̃ń/, 'He is at the hospital in Accra' must have the relative pronoun /áà/ and a subject with the second /wɔ/. Speakers of English often make the error of omitting /áà ɛ-/. Question and Answer Drill A, sentence 6.

4. Clauses beginning with conjunctions usually occur after another clause. If a clause beginning with a conjunction occurs first in a sentence, then it has slightly more emphasis.

5. /Ná mɪnɪ̄m sɛ́ɛ̀ ɔwɔ hɔ́/ is either 'I <u>know</u> or <u>knew</u> he was there'. (Lexical Drill A, sentence 10.)

6. In Pattern Drill A, the perfect followed by the consecutive of /w̃ɪé/, 'finish' is used to express completion, e.g., /Mɑ̀dɪ́dɪ àw̃ɪe/, 'I have finished eating', literally 'I have eaten to finish'. In Pattern Drill B, the perfect of /w̃ɪé/ followed by verbal noun is used to express completion, e.g., /Mɑ̀w̃ɪè ɑ̀dɪdɪ́/, 'I have finished eating'.

Verbal nouns are marked by a low-tone /a- ~ a-/ prefix to the verb stem which has the same tones as the simple present. There are also compound verbal nouns, which are composed of a noun plus a verb, e.g., /ɑ̀dwúmayɛ/, 'working', literally 'work-doing'. In compound verbal nouns, there is no /a- ~ ɑ-/ prefix unless the noun of the compound has this prefix in isolation. Compare the examples in Unit 7, Question and Answer Drill B.

Immediate past is expressed by adding /séèseì/ or /séèseì áà/ to these constructions, e.g., /Mɑ̀w̃ɪè ɑ̀dɪdɪ́ séèseì/, 'I have just eaten', or /Mɑ̀w̃ɪè ɑ̀dɪdɪ́ séèseì áà/, 'I have eaten just now'. If /áà/ occurs, the time elapsed between the completion of the action and the present is even less than that when /séèseì/ alone is used.

7. Indirect quotation of commands is expressed by the subjunctive
if the command is positive; but if the command is negative, the
present negative is used in the first and third persons and the
imperative negative in the second person, e.g., /Ɔsέ mέṇkɔ́/,
'He said I shouldn't go', /Ɔsέ ɛ̇ṇkɔ́/, 'He said you shouldn't go',
/ɔse ɔ́ṇkɔ́/, 'He said he shouldn't go'. See Pattern Drill C.

8. /tɛ̧/, 'to be sitting', 'to be dwelling or living', 'to exist',
is a stative verb and occurs only in the present or simple stem
and with /ná/.

     /tɛ̧ná/, /tɛ̧rá/, 'to sit down', 'come to a sitting position',
'live', 'stay', 'remain' is usually employed if a starting or
ending point is indicated.

     Compare sentence 3 and 6 of Question and Answer Drill B.
Sentence 6 employs /tɛ̧/ to refer to an existing condition with no
reference to beginning or end; but sentence 3 uses /tɛ̧ná/ to refer
to a specific period, viz., from the time you began to live here
until the present. /tɛ̧ná/ also is used to describe temporary
location, i.e., 'to remain', 'stay', and conditions which do not
obtain at the present, e.g., 'used to live', 'will sit'. See
also Question and Answer Drill B, sentence 10.

9. If there is an emphatic word or phrase followed by /na/ at
the beginning of the sentence, /ná/ indicating past tense and/or
emphasis for the verb comes after /na/ and not initially as is
the usual case. See Question and Answer Drill B, sentences
4 and 5.

10. In Twi, as in English, initial position in the sentence is
the position of prominence. Any element which is to be emphasized
can be moved to the beginning of the sentence and /na/ placed
after it to give it prominence. Compare /Wɔtɛ̧ há/, 'They live
here', and /Ɛhá na wɔtɛ̧/, 'Here /is where/ they live'; in the
second example here is emphasized.

11. /ɛhɛ́na/ is an interrogative personal pronoun, and it is only
used to ask questions. /nɛa/ is a relative pronoun or conjunction
meaning, 'the one who', 'the one that', 'he who', 'he whose',
'where', and is used to introduce relative clauses. Compare the
question and answer of Question and Answer Drill B, sentence 9.
See also Unit 6, Lexical Drill F.

12. /asɛ/ when the last element of a nominal compound also means
'the time of or during', e.g., /mmɔfáraasɛ̀/, 'childhood', 'the
time when a child'.

13. Most nouns with a low prefix and a high first stem vowel have
a high prefix and low stem vowel when occurring after a high tone
verb, e.g., /ɔyɛ́ ɑ́dùma/, 'He works'.

Unit 12

Basic Dialogue

-A-

| bɔ | to hit, strike |
| 1   Abɔ́ sɛ̃ń? | What time is it? |

-B-

ɔdóŋ (nòŋ) (pl. n-)	bell
nsíá̰	six
2 Abɔ́ nnón nsíá̰.	It is six o'clock.

-A-

| ɛy(ɛ́) áà | usually |
| 3   Ɛy(ɛ́) áà bɛ́rɛ̰ bɛ̃n n(a̰) ɔbá? | When does he come? |

-B-

dáa	always
pa	to pass by, move along
mɛ́nɛ̰tɛ̰́, mɛ́rɛ̰tɛ̰́ (pl. m-)	minute
a̰duonu	twenty
4 Ɔbá dáa nnón nsíá̰ ápà hɔ̃́ mmɛ́rɛ̰tɛ̰́ a̰duonũ.	He always comes at 6:20.

-A-

| gyina | to stand still, stop, halt |
| 5   Ɛdɛ̰ɛ̃́n ntí na ɛy(ɛ) áà ɛmã́ ogyiná wɔ há? | Why does he stop here? |

107

-B-

6   Ogyɪná wɔ há dɪdí.   He stops here and eats.

-A-

7   Odí mmɛ́r(ɛ̞) áhɛ̀?   How long does he stay?

-B-

8   Odí béyɛ mmɛ́rɛ̞tɛ̞ dúnnṳ̀m   He stays about fifteen minutes.

Notes

1. In a number of words /n/ alternates with /r/ between vowels,
as in /mɛ́nɛ̞tɛ̞/ or /mɛ́rɛ̞tɛ̞/ and /tɛ̞ná/ or /tɛ̞rá/.

2. Another common word for 'minute' is /sɪmmá/. /mɛ́nɛ̞tɛ̞/ is
// mɪnɪtɪ//.

3. /gyɪna/ is not followed by the consecutive form, e.g., /Ogyɪna
wɔ há dɪdɪ/, 'He stops here and eats'.

4. One of the meanings of /yɛ/, 'to be', is 'to amount to', 'come
to', 'total to', e.g., /wɔyɛ dú/, 'There are ten of them'. Though
/yɛ/ is a stative verb, it does have a future form, which has a
specialized meaning of 'about', 'approximately', e.g., /wɔbéyɛ
dú/, 'There are about ten of them'; however, if a price is quoted,
/béyɛ/ does not mean 'approximately', but 'the total is'.

Lexical Drill A

baakɔ́, bɪ̯akɔ́	1
mmɪenú, ɑ̞bɪeń	2
mmɪensá, abɪɛsá	3
ɛnnán	4
enúm	5

ensíá̧	6
ɛnsóŋ	7
ɛŋwɔtwȩ́	8
°ɛŋkɔróŋ	9
edú	10
dúbàakó	11
dúmienú	12
dúmiensá	13
dúnnáñ	14
dúnnúm	15
dúnsía	16
dúnsóŋ	17
dúŋwɔtwȩ́	18
dúŋkɔróŋ	19
a̧duonú	20
°a̧duonúbàakó	21
a̧duonúmienú	22
a̧duonúmiensá	23
a̧duonúnáñ	24
a̧duonúnúm	25
a̧duonúnsía̧	26
a̧duonúnsóŋ	27
a̧duonúŋwɔtwę̧	28
a̧duonúŋkɔróŋ	29
a̧dua̧sá	30
a̧dua̧náñ	40

109

ạduonŭm	50
ạduosĩá	60
ạduosôŋ	70
ạduowótwẹ	80
ạduokọrôŋ	90
ɔha	100
ɔhá nẹ́ baakɛ́	101
ɔhá nẹ́ dú	110
ạhạạnŭ	200
apẹ́m (pl. m-)	1000

Pattern Drill A

Read the numbers horizontally.

a.				b.			
18	80	28		40	50	4	5
17	70	27		14	15	45	54
16	60	26		60	70	6	7
15	50	25		16	17	67	76
14	40	24		20	30	2	3

c.				d.			
19	90	29		36	63	33	66
16	15	13		25	52	22	55
20	50	40		67	76	77	66
25	22	27		19	99	9	11
38	68	18		8	88	38	78

e. 200   102   202   f.   200   300   400

    600   604   640   1500   1600   1700

    317   307   371   1808   1919   2000

    869   879   829   1962   2116   2473

    403   402   430   7847   5353   4962

Lexical Drill B

1. Baakó (έ)né baakó yɛ mmıenú.   1 and 1 ıs   2

2. Mmıenú né mmıenú yɛ nnáñ.   2 and 2 ıs   4

3. Mmıensá né mmıensá yɛ nsíá.   3 and 3 ıs   6

4. Ɛnnáñ né nnáñ yɛ ŋwotwé.   4 and 4 ıs   8

5. Enúm né enúm yɛ dú.   5 and 5 ıs 10

6. Ensíá né nsíá yɛ dúmìenú.   6 and 6 ıs 12

7. Ɛnsón né nsón yɛ dúnáñ.   7 and 7 ıs 14

8. Cụwɔtwé nó ŋwɔtwé yɛ dúnsíạ.   8 and 8 ıs 16

9. Ɛnkọrón né nkọrón yɛ dúŋwòtwɛ.   9 and 9 ıs 18

10. Edú né dú yɛ ạduonu.   10 and 10 ıs 20

Lexical Drill C

1. Wóyì mmıensá fırı ensíá mú áà,   6 mınus 3 ıs 3
    ɛká mmıensá.   ('When three is
    from sıx's whole, ıt remaıns
    three.')

2. Wóyì dú fırı ạduạsá mú áà,   30 mınus 10 ıs 20
    ɛká ạduonu.

3. Wóyì nnáñ fırı ɛnkọrón mú áà,   9 mınus 4 ıs 5
    ɛká enúm.

111

4. Wóyì ŋwɔtwɛ́ fırı dúmìenú mú áà,   12 mınus 8 ıs 4
    ɛká ɛnnáñ.

5. Wóyì nsíá fırı dúnsóŋ mú áà,   17 mınus 6 ıs 11
    ɛká dúbàakɔ́.

6. Wóyì dúnúm fırı ạduonú mú áà,   20 mınus 15 ıs 5
    ɛká enúm.

7. Wóyì ŋwɔtwɛ́ fırı ạduonúnáñ mú   24 mınus 8 ıs 16
    áà, ɛká dúnsíá.

8. Wóyì ạduosíá fırı ạduosóŋ mú áà,   70 mınus 60 ıs 10
    ɛká edú.

9. Wóyì ạduạnánnán fırı dúbàakɔ́ mú   44 mınus 11 ıs 33
    áà, ɛká ạduạsámiensã.

10. Wóyì ạduosíáŋwòtwɛ fırı ạduosóŋ   70 mınus 68 ıs 2
    mú áà, ɛká mmıenú.

New words

   /(Sɛ)....áà/   See note 7.

   ka   to remaın, be left

Question and Answer Drıll A

1. Mfíe áhɛ̀ ní áà wɔ̣bɛtɛ̣rãa   How many years has ıt been
    há?   sınce you lıved here?

    Mfíe dú ní áà mɛ̃bɛ́terãa   It has been ten years
    há.   sınce I have lıved here.

2. Mfíe áhě ní áà ɔkɔɔ   How long ago did he leave
   Amɛ́rɛ̀ka?   for America?
   Ɔkɔɔ Amɛ́rɛ̀ka mfíe nǎñ   He left for America four
   ní.   years ago.

3. Ebédɪ mfíe áhě na wɔ́bɛsáñ   How long will it be until
   ábà Ghánà?   you return to Ghana?
   Médɪ mfíe mmɪenú ansáà   It will be two years
   na méba Ghánà.   until I return to Ghana.

4. Nnípa ahɛ́ na ɛwɔ dǎñ mú   How many people are there
   hó?   in that room?
   Wɔbɛ́yɛ nnípa ạduạnúm na   There are about fifty
   ɛwɔ dǎñ mú hó.   people in that room.

5. Nnípa áhě pɛ́ n(a) ɛɛbá?   Exactly how many are coming?
   Wɔbɛ́yɛ ạduạnúm pɛ́pɛɛpɛ   There will be exactly
   na ɛɛbá.   fifty.

6. Sɪká áhě na wɔ́wɔ̀?   How much money do you have?
   Mɛ̃wɔ pón baakó pɛ́.   I have exactly one pound.

7. Efí Ŋkɛrǎñ kó Kumásɛ bɛ́yɛ   How many miles is it from
   akwáñsíñ áhě?   Accra to Kumasi?
   Efí Ŋkɛrǎñ kó Kumásɛ   It's about 120 miles from
   ɛbɛ́yɛ akwáñsíñ ɔhá ní   Accra to Kumasi.
   ạduonú.

113

8. Sɛ wúfì Ŋkɛṛã́ñ Kumásɛ   How long does ıt take to
    áà, edí mmɛ́r(ɛ) áhɛ̀?   get from Accra to Kumasɪ?
    Sɛ wúfì Ŋkɛṛã́ñ rɛkɔ   It takes nıne hours from
    Kumásɛ áà, <u>edí</u>   Accra to Kuması.
    <u>nnɔnhwɛ́rɛ́w ŋkɔrɔ́n.</u>

9. Wúgyınaà há ákyɛ̀?   How long have you been
                     standing here?

    Mạgyína há <u>mmɛ́rɛ̀tɛ́</u>   I've been standing only
    <u>nṹm pɛ́.</u>   fıve mınutes.

10. Wɔtɛnã́à há ákyɛ̀?   How long have you been waıtıng?

    Matɛ́nã́ há <u>mmɛ́rɛ̀tɛ́</u>   I've only been waıtıng some
    <u>nṹm ní.</u>   fıve mınutes.

New words

     nɛ   to be, (See note 6.)

     betɛ̣ṛã́   to come, sıt down; settle,
                                    take up a habıtatıon

     pɛ́   exactly, only, precısely,
                                    thoroughly

     ɔkwã́ñ (pl. a-)   road, path; way, method;
                                    opportunıty

     esíṇ (pl. ạsıṇsíṇ)   part, pıece, fragment,
                                    remnant

     ɔkwã́nsíṇ (pl. a-)   mıle

     tɛ̣rɛ́ṇ   traın

     hwɛ̣rɛ́   to consume, use up, pass
                                    tıme

| doŋhwérę́w (pl. n-) | hour |
| kyε | to continue, endure, last |

Pattern Drill B

Nnón mmıenú ábɔ̀ ápà hɔ́ mmę́nę̀tę́   It's 2:15. It's fifteen
dúnnúm.   after two.

Read the following tımes ın Twı.

6:20	10:45
5:10	11:55
2:00	7:35
4:05	2:10
12:30	6:25
7:15	12:50
8:40	9:00
9:50	4:30
1:05	5:45
3:35	3:50

Pattern Drill C

Aká mmę́rę̀tę́ dú na y(ε) ábɔ̀   It's ten mınutes untıl one.
dóŋ kɔrɔ.

Read the following tımes ın Twı.

1:35	2:53
11:50	6:33
7:45	10:45
8:55	3:57
9:42	4:50

5. Compound numerals are written in the orthography as two words;
but they are written here as one word because they are compounds
as shown by their tone sandhi, i.e., tone differences which occur
in combination, e.g., /a̧duonúbàakó/ is // aduonu baako//. Tone
sandhi of compounds will be discussed in detail in a later chapter.

Compound numerals between thirty and one hundred have the
same tone pattern as that used in combination with twenty, i.e.,
/a̧duonú/. See Lexical Drill A.

6. /(ɛ)nkǫróŋ/ is // nkron//.

7. /sɛ/ at the beginning of a clause followed by /àá/ at the end
of a clause means, 'if', 'when', 'whenever', 'on the occasion
that'. Quite often the /sɛ/ is omitted, but the meaning is still
the same.

8. /ní/ is a contraction of /nę eyí/, 'is this', e.g., /Pɛnsęrę
ní/, 'Here is a pencil', 'This is a pencil'. See also Question
and Answer Drill A, sentences one and two.

/nę nǒ/ contracts to /nęŋ/.

/nę/ means 'to be', 'consist of', 'be identical with', e.g.,
/Ɔnę́ kɛsę́ɛ/, 'He is great', 'He is the great one', (and no other
is as great); but /oyɛ́ kɛsę́ɛ/, 'He is great', (and there are also
others who are as great).

9. /dóŋ kǫrǫ/ and /dóŋ kǫ/ are alternate forms of /dóŋ baakó/.

Unit 13

Basic Dialogue

-A-

ɔbɔ́ɔ (bɔ́ɔ) (pl. a-)   price; stone; kernel, seed

1 Né bɔ́ɔ y(ɛ) ahɛ́?   How much is this?

-B-

°sírɛ̀ŋ   shilling

2 Né bɔ́ɔ yɛ sírɛ̀ŋ mmienú.   It's 2 shillings.

-A-

búùku, búùkuú   book

kɔkɔɔ́   red

3 Búùku kɔkɔɔ́ nɔ̃́ y(ɛ) ahɛ́?   How much is this red book?

-B-

4 Pɔ́n baakɔ̃́ ní sírɔ̀ŋ dú.   One pound and ten shillings.

-A-

fa   to take, grasp, seize

5 Fa ɛnɔ̃́ mɛ́ mɛ̃.   Give me that one.

akɔ́kɔsɛràdɛ́ɛ   yellow

kɛ́raàtaá (pl. ŋ-)   paper

6 Mɛ́ mɛ̃ akɔ́kɔsɛràdɛ́ɛ kɛ́raàtaá   Give me some yellow paper too.
   ńsɔ bí.

-B-

hwɛhwɛ́   to look for, look after

7 Ahɛ́ na wɔ́hwɛ̀hwɛ́?   How much do you want?

117

-A-

bǫaá	bundle, bunch
8 Má mɛ̃ bǫaá.	Give me a package.
ɲyɪ̃nᵃa	all
ní ɲyɪ̃nᵃa	all of it
9 Ní ɲyɪ̃nᵃa bǫo bɛ́yɛ ahɛ̃?	How much is the total price?

-B-

| 10 Ní ɲyɪ̃nᵃa bǫo bɛ́yɛ póŋ mmɪenú. | That will be 2 pounds altogether. |

Notes

1. /Nɛ̃ bǫo ahɛ̃?/, 'How much /is/ this?', is also very common.

2. /síreŋ/ is often /síre̩/ or /sɛ́rɛ̀/ and is //srɛ//.

3. Languages divide up the color spectrum in different ways. These are the most common color terms with their approximate equivalents in English:

kɔkɔó	red, reddish or chocolate brown, orange, purple
tuntumí	black; dark shades of blue, green, brown, gray, or tan; very dark red
fítaa	white, (clear)
fúfuo	white
akǫkoseradéɛ	yellow, light tan
ahabãmmónõ	green
°bíruù	blue

/kokɔɔ́/, /tuntúm/, /fítaa/, and /fúfuo/ are adjectives and
follow their nouns, as other adjectives do. /akɔ́kosɛràdéɛ/ and
/ahabãmmóñõ/ are compound nouns and precede their nouns. /akɔ́kɔ̀/,
'chicken' plus /sɛradéɛ̀/, 'fat', 'grease' indicates 'the color of
hen's fat', i.e., 'yellow'. /ahabáñ/, 'leaf', 'foilage', plus
/amóñõ/, 'fresh', 'green', 'unripe', indicates 'the color of
fresh leaves', i.e., 'green'.
      Light shades are indicated by a following /ᵒkakɛrá/, 'little',
'small', e.g., /ahabãmmóñõ kakɛrá/, 'light green'. With adjectives
only, reduplication is used to indicate dark shades, e.g.,
/tuntuuntúm/, 'very black', /fıtɑ̀fıta/, 'very white', /kokɔɔko/,
'brilliant red', 'dark red'. The double vowel may be lengthened
to several times its usual length to show more intensity of color.
The longer the vowel, the darker or more intense the color.

4. /akɔ́kosɛràdéɛ/ is // akoksrade//.
    /kɛ́raàtaá/ is // kraataa//.
    /ní/, 'and', 'with', is // ne//.
    /kakɛrá/ is // kakra//.
    /bíruù/ is // bruu//.

    Question and Answer Drill A

    1. Nɛ́ bɔ̀ɔ yɛ sɛ́ñ?   How much is this?
        Nɛ́ bɔ̀ɔ yɛ tɑkú.   It is a sixpence.
    2. Ŋhómã yí bɔ̀ɔ yɛ sɛ́ñ?   How much is this book?
        Ŋhómã yí bɔ̀ɔ yɛ póŋ   This book is one pound.
        kó.
    3. Ntámã́ yí bɔ̀ɔ yɛ sɛ́ñ?   How much is this ntama?
        Ntamã́ yí bɔ̀ɔ yɛ póŋ   This ntama is three pounds.
        mmiensá.

4. Pénsęrę yí bǫ́ɔ yɛ sɛ́ñ?   How much ıs thıs pencıl?

    Pénsęrę yí bǫ́ɔ yɛ   Thıs pencıl ıs a threepence.
    tǫró.

5. Ɔpǫ́ñ yí bǫ́ɔ yɛ sɛ́ñ?   How much ıs thıs table?

    Ɔpǫ́ñ yí bǫ́ɔ yɛ pón   Thıs table ıs ten pounds.
    dú.

6. Kę́raàtaá yí bǫ́ɔ yɛ sɛ́ñ?   How much ıs thıs paper?

    Kę́raàtaá yí bǫ́ɔ yɛ   Thıs paper ıs a sıxpence.
    sęmpǫá.

7. Ɔsę́kàñ yí bǫ́ɔ yɛ sɛ́ñ?   How much ıs thıs knıfe?

    Ɔsę́kàñ yí bǫ́ɔ yɛ pón   Thıs knıfe ıs three pounds.
    mmıensá.

8. Kyóɔku yí bǫ́ɔ yɛ sɛ́ñ?   How much ıs thıs chalk?

    Kyóɔku yí bǫ́ɔ yɛ   Thıs chalk ıs a sıxpence.
    tąkufá.

9. Ofíe yí bǫ́ɔ yɛ sɛ́ñ?   How much ıs thıs house?

    Ofíe yí bǫ́ɔ yɛ pón   Thıs house ıs 5,000 pounds.
    pę́m núm.

10. Ɛdóñ yí bǫ́ɔ yɛ sɛ́ñ?   How much ıs thıs bell?

    Ɛdóñ yí bǫ́ɔ yɛ sírèn   Thıs bell ıs thırty shıllıngs.
    ąduąsá.

New words

opóŋ (pl. a-)   door, gate; table, desk;
                                   meal, feast

osékáñ (sékáñ) (pl. a-)   knife, razor

kyóòku, kyóòkǫ   chalk

tąkú, tąkufá (pl. n-)   sixpence

tǫró, tęró   threepence

sęmpǫá   sixpence

kápèrɛ   penny

Question and Answer Drill B

1. Wúdìì na ahé wo   How long did you spend in
   Ąburokyírı?   Europe?
   Mídıı mfie náñ wo   I spent four years in
   Ąburokyírı.   Europe.

2. Wàkò Ąburokyírı péŋ?   Have you been to Europe before?
   Dąąbí, mèŋkóò   No, I have never been to
   Ąburokyírı péŋ.   Europe?

3. Wúbeduùyɛ nó, ná abó   What time was it when you
   ahé?   arrived?
   Míbéduruùyɛ nó, ná   It was half past one when
   yabó dóŋ kǫrǫ́ né fá.   I arrived.

4. Ɛdęén ntí na wǫ́sáñ   Why did you come back?
   baayɛ?
   Mésáñ baay séè míbehú   I came back to see you.
   wǫ.

121

5. Mmá áhề na w(ɔ́) awɔ́fɔɔ wɔ?

How many other children do your parents have?

   Máwɔfɔɔ wɔ <u>mmá mmiensá̃ ńsɔ.</u>

My parents have three other children.

6. Mfíe áhề ní áà wátɛ̨rã̃ há̃?

How many years have you lived here?

   Matɛ̨rã̃ há̃ <u>mfíe nsɔ́n̩ ní.</u>

I have lived here for seven years.

7. Sɛ odidí áà edí mmɛ́r(ɛ) ahɛ̃́?

How long does he take to eat?

   Sɛ odidí áà ɔtaá ɛ̨́dì <u>mmɛ́rɛ̨tɛ̨ dúnṹm.</u>

He often takes fifteen minutes to eat.

8. Mfíe áhề na wɔ́ papá ɛ̨́dì?

How old is your father?

   Mɛ̃́ papá ɛ̨dí <u>mfíe aduonṹnṹm.</u>

My father is fifty-five years old.

9. Ahɛ̃́ na wɔ́sɛ̃ɛ̃ wɔ sɔ́tɔɔ̀ mũ̃́ hó?

How much did you spend in that store?

   Mɔ̃sɛ̃ɛ̃ <u>sírɛ̀n̩ dúnnã́ñ pɛ̃́.</u>

I spent only fourteen shillings.

10. Nnípa áhề na éhyiɑ̨̀ɑ̨̀ wɔ sukúù mũ̃́ hó?

How many people met at the school?

   <u>Nnípa bɛ́yɛ ɔhá na</u> éhyiɑ̨̀ɑ̨̀ wɔ sukúù mũ̃́ hó.

About a hundred people met at the school.

New words

Ąburokyírı	Europe, America
pếŋ	once, one tıme, ever, before
du, duru	to arrıve, reach; be sufficient
awǫ́fǫɔ, awǫ́fǫnõm	parents
taá	to pursue, chase, follow; do often or repeatedly
sɛɛ	to use up, spend; destroy, mar, ruın
hyıá̧	to meet, assemble; agree, be ın accord

Pattern Drıll A

1. Búùku kḗtęwaa tuntum̃ da
   opṍnõ nǿ sǫ́.

   A small black book ıs lyıng on the table.

2. Pénsę̀rę tḗńtḗn ḱokɔɔ́ ɔ̀a
   opṍnõ nǿ sǫ́.

   A long red pencıl ıs lyıng on the table.

3. Pénsę̀rę tḗńtḗn kokɔɔ́ nǿ
   yɛ mḗ dę̀a.

   The long red pencıl ıs mıne.

4. Ahabắmmṍnõ káà fǫ́fǫ̀rǫ
   nǿ yɛ mḗ dę̀a.

   That new green car ıs mıne.

5. Ahabắmmṍnõ káà fǫ́fǫ̀rǫ
   nǿ fırı Ąburokyírı.

   That new green car ıs from Europe.

6. °Ataadę́ɛ dédą̀w fítaa yí
   fırı Ąburokyírı.

   Thıs old whıte dress came from Europe.

7. Ataadę́ɛ dédą̀w fítaa yí
   ñyɛ́.

   Thıs old whıte dress ıs no good.

8. <u>Mɛ́ sɛ̨kǎn fɔ́fɔ́rɔ̨ kɛsɛ̨́ɛ</u>   My other big knife is no good.
<u>nɔ́ ñyɛ́.</u>

9. Mɛ́ sɛ̨kǎn fɔ́fɔ́rɔ̨ kɛsɛ̨́ɛ   My other big knife is outside.
nɔ́ <u>wɔ abɔntɛ̨́ñ.</u>

10. °Ɔkɛ́rǎmǎñ kɛsɛ̨́ɛ kokoó   The big light-brown dog is
kakɛ̨rá wɔ abɔntɛ̨́ñ.   outside.

New words

kɛ̨tɛ̨wa (pl. ŋ-)	small, little
tɛ̨́ntɛ̨ñ	long, high, tall
°ataadɛ̨́ɛ	clothes
kɛsɛ̨́ɛ (pl. a-)	big, large; great, grand
abɔntɛ̨́ñ (pl. m-)	street
dédàw	old, ancient
ɔkɛ́rǎmǎñ (pl. a-)	dog

Pattern Drill B

1. Ɛdɛ̨ɛ́n ntí na wúkoò fíe?   Why did you go home?
2. Ɛdɛ̨ɛ́n ntí na wánkò fíe?   Why didn't you go home?
3. Ɛdɛ̨ɛ́n ntí na wóbaày?   Why did you come?
4. Ɛdɛ̨ɛ́n ntí na wámmá?   Why didn't you come?
5. Ɛdɛ̨ɛ́n ntí na wótɔɔ́y?   Why did you buy it?
6. Ɛdɛ̨ɛ́n ntí na wántɔ̀?   Why didn't you buy it?
7. Ɛdɛ̨ɛ́n ntí na wúbisaà nɔ́?   Why did you ask him?
8. Ɛdɛ̨ɛ́n ntí na wámmisa nɔ́?   Why didn't you ask him?
9. Ɛdɛ̨ɛ́n ntí na wókǎà saá?   Why did you say that?
10. Ɛdɛ̨ɛ́n ntí na wánkǎ saá?   Why didn't you say so?

New words

     sa, saá   so, thus, in that manner

Question and Answer Drill C

1. Mfíe áhè na ná mádɪ   How old were you when you
   mmę́r(ę) áà mɔ́baà   came to America?
   Amę́rę̀ka?
   <u>Ná mądí mfíe dúnnáñ</u>   I was fourteen when we came
   mmę́r(ę) áà yɛbáà   to America.
   Amę́rę̀ka?

2. Pépà ahɛ̂ na wɔ́ɔhwę̀hwɛ? How much paper do you want?
   Mɛ̃́ɛ̃hwę̀hwɛ́ <u>pépà sírèɲ</u> I want a shilling's worth of
   <u>átɔ̀</u>.   paper.

3. Sírɔ̀ɲ bɛ́tɔ pépà ahɛ́?   How much paper will a shilling
                    buy?
   Sírę̀ɲ bɛ́tɔ pépà <u>adákà</u> A shilling will buy one box
   <u>baakɔ́</u>.   of paper.

4. Ebédɪ mmę́r(ę) áhɛ̃ ansɛ́ How long will it be until he
   na ɔbɛ́sɛ́ñ ábà?   gets back?
   <u>Ebédɪ bɛ́yɛ nnɔ́ɲhwę́rę̀w</u> It will be about two hours
   <u>mmɪenṹ</u> ansɛ́ na   until he gets back.
   ɔbɛ́sɛ́ñ ábà.

5. Ehíą́ mɛ́ wɔ nnípa ahɛ̃? How many people do you need?
   Ehíą́ mɛ́ <u>mɛ̃ nnípa</u>   I need a few more people.
   <u>kétewąą bí</u>.

6. Ehĩá̃ mã́ wǫ nnípa áhɛ̃̀   How many more people do you
      bío?   need?

   Ehĩá̃ mã́ mɛ̃ nnípa nsĩá   I need six more people.
      bío.

7. Sɪká̃ ahɛ̃́ na ehĩá̃ mã́w?   How much money do you need?

   Ehĩá̃ mã́ mɛ̃ sírɛ̀ɲ   I need two shillings.
      mmɪenú̃.

8. Mmɛ̃́rɛ̨ bɛ̃́n na ofí ą́dwùma   When does he start to work?
      asɛ̨?

   Ofí ą́dwùma asɛ̨ nnón   He starts to work at ten
      dú.   o'clock.

9. Mmɛ̃́rɛ̨ bɛ̃́n na ɔpɔ́ɲ   When does he quit work?
      ą́dwùma?

   Ɔpɔ̃́ɲ ą́dwùma nnón nsĩą́   He quits work at six thirty.
      nɛ̃́ fã́.

10. Dá bɛ̃́ɲ na ɛyɛ́ áà wǫ́kɔ   What days do you go there?
      hó?

    Mɛ̃kó hó dáa.   I go there every day.

11. Wǫ́tàá kó hó dáa?   How often do you go there?

    Nnawótwɛ̨ bɪ̨ara mɛ̃kó   I go there three times a
      hó nnansá̃.   week.

New words

      pépà   paper

      adáká   box, case, trunk, suitcase

      hĩá̃   to distress, trouble, need,
                                 require

126

fı...asę	to begin, start
póṇ	to go away, cease, stop; disjoin, separate
nnawótwę	week
bıara	each, every
nnansá	three days
dáa	always, ever, continually, every day

Pattern Drill C

1. Sɛ wúñyá̰ w̌ıé pé áà, berá mĩ fíe.
   As soon as you finish, come to my house.

2. Sɛ wúñyá̰ w̌ıé pé áà, kotó borodo má̰ mě.
   As soon as you finish, go buy some bread.

3. Sɛ wúwò sıká áà, kotó borodo má̰ mě.
   If you have any money, go buy me some bread.

4. Sɛ wúwò sıká áà, tuá mpá nǒ ká má̰ mě.
   If you have the money pay me for the bed.

5. Kyẹrɛ nǒ má̰ óntuą mpá nǒ ká má̰ mě.
   Tell him to pay me for the bed.

6. Kyẹrɛ nǒ má̰ óṇko fíe.
   Tell him to go home.

7. Bısa nǒ má̰ óṇko fíe.
   Ask him to go home.

8. Bısa nǒ má̰ óntuą mě ká.
   Ask him to pay me.

9. Oññyá̰ ntúą̀ą̀ mě ká.
   He hasn't paid me yet.

10. Oññyá̰ mmaayɛ.
    He hasn't come yet.

127

New words

ɛká (pl. ŋ̩-)	debt, something which is lacking
tuạ	to pay, repay, fill up, replace
ñyậ	to get, acquire, receive, obtain

5. /ɔpóŋ̩ yí/ is /ɔpóñ yí/, i.e., before /y/, /n/ and /ŋ/ are replaced by /ñ/. /ɔpónɔ́/, means only 'table', 'desk', and is often used if /ɔpóŋ̩/ is not clear from the context.

6. /nɔ́/, 'that', and /yí/, 'this', at the end of an adverbial clause mark the contraction of a longer clause, e.g., /wúbeduùyɛ nɔ́/, 'when you arrived', is a contraction of /mmɛ́r(ę) áà wúbeduùyɛ mɔ́/, 'the time /at/ which you arrived'.

7. /taá/ 'to pursue', 'follow', when followed by another verb means 'to do often or repeatedly'.

8. /dęa/ is the same as /nęa/.

9. A few adjectives have plurals. /kę́tęwa/ has plural /ŋkę́tęwa/. /kę́tęwaa/ is an intensive form, i.e., 'very small'.

10. /ataadę́ɛ/ is often /átadé/. /ataadę́ɛ/ refers to clothes which are tailored to fit the body in contrast to /ntãmá/ which are wrapped or draped around the body.

11. /wɔ abontéñ/ is literally 'to be on the street', but it is often used to mean 'outside', 'not indoors'. Also used in this way are /ądɪ/, 'out', 'outside', 'outdoors', 'abroad', and /ądíwo/, 'the yard around a house', 'outside', 'outdoors'.

12.   /ɔkɛ́rámáñ/ ıs /ɔkraman/.

13.   /ɛdɛ̥ɛ́ñ ntí/ ıs often /ɛdɛ̥ɛ́n ntí/, ı.e., /ñ̥/ ıs usually /n/
before /n/.

14.   /sɛ ñyã́...áà/ has the sıgnıfıcance 'as soon as'. The
negatıve of /ñyã́/ when precedıng another verb means 'not yet'.

Unit 14

Basic Dialogue

-A-

1 °Tɛlɛfɔ́n nɔ́ rɛbɔ́. Kotíe   The phone is ringing. Answer
      tɛlɛfɔ́n nɔ́.   the phone.

-B-

      tíe   to hear, listen
2 Hɛ́lɔ̀, mɛ̃ Owúsù na, mɛ̃ekasa   Hello, Owusu speaking.
      yí.

-C-

3 Yǫǫ, kasa na mĩ́ıtíe wǫ; ɛyɛ   Yes, I hear you; this is Abenaa
      mɛ̃́ Ábɛnaa Asantɛwa.   Asantewa.

-B-

4 Na wamáné̩ɛ?   What can I do for you?

-C-

      síesìe   to repair, fix, arrange,
                                             prepare

      bą̀ąbí (pl. -nǫm)   a place, somewhere
5 Ɛhɛ̃́fá̃ na mĩ́ñyã̃ bą̀ąbí ná   Where can I find a place to get
      yá̩sıesìe mɛ̃ káà nɔ́?   my car fixed?

-B-

      ŋkwantá   crossroad, junction, a 'Y'
6 Bą̀ąbı pápa wɔ Kégyetìą   There's a good place at Kegyetia
      Ŋkwantá.   Crossroad.

130

-C-

7   Mɛ̆da wasę.   Thank you.

-B-

8   Mmɛ́ ɛnná asę.   You're welcome. Don't mention it.

Notes

1. Telephone numbers are usually given in English in Ghana.   If
given in English, the numbers are said in groups of two, e.g.,
3578 is thirty-five, seventy-eight.   If given in Twi, 3578 would
be said like this: /mpę́m miensá ahá nûm nɛ́ ąduosɔ̃ŋ ŋwɔtwę́/.

2. English words are quite common in Twi.   Words that were
borrowed some time ago have been modified so that they now fit
the structure of the Twi sound system, e.g., /sírę̀ŋ/, 'shilling'.
Initial l was interpreted as /d/, and l in other positions was
interpreted as /r/.   /l/ is now commonly used in words, recently
borrowed, such as /ntílý/ and /lɛlątfɔ́n/.   English words are often
spelled in English fashion, but also they may be spelled as they
are pronounced in Twi.   Common words may be spelled both ways,
e.g., /káȧ/ is both // kaa// and // car//.   If English spelling isn't
used, word-final consonants are either dropped or a vowel is added
after them.   Consonant clusters either lose a consonant or a vowel
is inserted between the consonants.   Double consonants lose a
letter.   The table below indicates how respelling is usually done.

English	Twi
c (if pronounced k)	k
ch (if pronounced k)	k
ch (if pronounced č)	ky
j	gy
ph	f

131

qu	kw
sh	s (also hy)
th	t
v	w
z	s

Even though a word is borrowed, it may be used only in some of the situations or with only some of the meanings that it has in English. For example, /hɛlò/ is regularly used on the telephone; but when greeting another person face to face, the customary Twi greetings are used nearly always.

3. /tɛlɛfón/ is // telefon//.

4. Notice the s-like sound between /t/ and /ɪ/ in /tɪe/.

Pattern Drill A

1. Ɛhéfá na mínyǎ bạạbí ná   Where can I find a place to
    yạsıesìe mɛ̃ káà nó?   get my car fixed?

2. Ɛhéfá na mínyǎ bạạbí ná   Where can I find a place to
    yáhọrò mɛ̃ ntáádẹɛ?   get my clothes washed?

3. Ɛhéfá na mínyǎ bạạbí ná   Where can I find a place to
    °yáhyạın mĭ °hyúù?   get my shoes shined?

4. Ɛhéfá na mínyǎ bạạbí ná   Where can I find a place to
    yạyì mĭ tí?   get my haircut?

5. Ɛhéfá na mínyǎ bạạbí átò   Where can I find a place to
    ạduạnẹ́ (ạdì)?   buy food?

Pattern Drill B

1. Ɛhɛ́rɛ́ na míñyɛ̨́ obí ná wɛ̨́sìesìe mɛ̃ káà nɔ́?	Where can I find someone to fix my car?
2. Ɛhɛ́rɛ́ na míñyɛ̨́ obí ná wáhɔ̀rɔ̨ mɛ̃ ntáádɛ̨ɛ?	Where can I find someone to wash my clothes?
3. Ɛhɛ́rɛ́ na míñyɛ̨́ obí ná °wɛ̨́hyɛ̨ìn mĩ °hyúù?	Where can I find someone to shine my shoes?
4. Ɛhɛ́rɛ́ na míñyɛ̨́ obí ná wɛ̨́yì mĩ tí?	Where can I find someone to cut my hair?
5. Ɛhɛ́rɛ́ na míñyɛ̨́ obí áà ɔtɔ́ɲ ɛ̨́dùɛ̨nɛ̨?	Where can I find someone who sells food?

Pattern Drill C

1. Bɛ̨ɛ̨bì pápa wo Kógyetìɛ̨ Ŋkwantá.	There's a good place at Kegyetia Crossroad.
2. Bɛ̨ɛ̨bì pápa wɔ kúrom.	There's a good place in town.
3. Bɛ̨ɛ̨bì pápa wɔ ɛ̨subɔntɛ́n nɔ́ ñkyɛ́ñ.	There's a good place by the river.
4. Bɛ̨ɛ̨bì pápa tɔa sìkakɔ́rabɛ̨adɛ̨́ñ nɔ́ sɔ́.	There's a good place adjoining the bank.
5. Bɛ̨ɛ̨bì pápa wɔ adɛ̨́ñ áà esí wɛ̨́nìm yí.	There's a good place in the building opposite us.

133

Pattern Drill D

1. Bąąbí nní há áà <u>yesiésìe</u>
   <u>káà</u>.

   There's no place here that
   repairs cars.

2. Bąąbí nní há áà <u>yɛhǫrǫ</u>
   <u>nnę́ɛma</u>.

   There's no place here that
   washes things.

3. Bąąbí nní há áà <u>yeyí tí</u>.

   There's no place here that
   gives haircuts.

4. Bąąbí nní há áà <u>yɛtǫ̀ǹ</u>
   <u>ąduąnę́</u>.

   There's no place here that
   sells food.

5. Bąąbí nní há áà <u>yɛyé</u>
   <u>pépà</u>.

   There's no place here that
   makes paper.

New words

hǫrǫ, hǫhǫ́rǫ	to wash
yɪ	to take away, remove; shave, cut the hair
obí (pl. -nõm)	someone, somebody, anybody, one
ąsubontẽ́ñ, ąsútẽñ (pl. n-)	river, stream
sɪkakǫ́rabę̀a	bank, safe, place to keep money
sɪkakǫ́rabę̀adáñ	bank, bank building
tǫa	to join, connect, bring together
ąní	eye; color
ąnìm	face, countenance; front; before, in front of

Lexical Drill A

1. Sɛ wúdu fíe áà, fɛrέ   As soon as you get home, call
   mɛ̃.   me.

2. Sɛ wúdu fíe áà, befɛrέ   As soon as you get home, come
   mɛ̃.   (over) and call me.

3. Sɛ wúwìe áà, befɛrέ mɛ̃.   When you finish, come (over)
                                and call me.

4. Sɛ wúwìe áà, fɛrέ nó   When you finish, phone him.
   wɔ tɛlɛfóń sɔ́.

5. Ansá na wúbèfɩ asɛ̨́ nó,   Before you start, call him.
   fɛrέ nó wɔ tɛlɛfóń sɔ́.

6. Ansá na wúbèfɩ asɛ̨́ nó,   Before you start, go call him.
   kɔfɛ̨́rɛ nó.

7. Sɛ tɛlɛfóń nó bɔ́ pέ áà,   If the telephone rings, go
   kɔfɛ̨́rɛ nó.   call him.

8. Sɛ tɛlɛfóń nó bɔ́ pέ áà,   If the telephone rings,
   tìe.   answer it.

9. Sɛ ɔbá bɛkasá áà, tìe   If he comes to talk, listen
   nó.   to him. (be patient with
                                him)

10. Sɛ ɔbá bɛkasá áà, fɛrέ   If he comes to talk, call me.
    mɛ̃.

Lexical Drill B

1. Kyɛrɛwpõn nõ yɛ mẽ dɛ̧a.   The desk is mine.

2. Kyɛrɛwpõn nõ si ofa̧sú   The desk is next to the wall.
   nõ hõ.

3. A̧kõññúa̧ nõ si ofa̧sú   The chair is by the wall.
   nõ hõ.

4. A̧kõññúa̧ nõ nní há.   The chair isn't here.

5. Abo̧fára nõ nní há.   The child isn't here.

6. Abo̧fára nõ da mpá nõ   The child is lying on the bed.
   so̧.

7. Safõwá nõ da mpá nõ so̧.   The key is lying on the bed.

8. Safõwá nõ tua̧ ɔpõn nõ   The key is in the lock.
   a̧ní.

9. Safõwá áà a̧bù tua̧ ɔpõn   There is a broken key in the
   nõ a̧ní.   lock.

10. Mĩtuu safõwá áà a̧bù nõ   I took the broken key out of
    fii ɔpõn nõ a̧ní.   the door.

New words

fi...asɛ̧   to begin

ofa̧sú (pl. a̧-)   wall

safõwá, sáfẽ (pl. n-)   key

tua̧   to stick at or in, be stuck
                               at or in

bu   to bend, curve; break, break
                               off, decide, judge

mpá   bed, couch, mattress

opốnạnɪ(wa)   lock, keyhole

ɛsǫ́   upper part or surface of;
                              on, upon, over, above

Lexical Drill C

1. Tɪe ɔkyɛrɛkyɛ́rɛfǫɔ nố.   Listen to the teacher.

2. Wốŋ ǻŋhǘ kyɛrɛkyɛ́rɛfǫɔ   They couldn't find the teacher.
   nố.

3. Wốŋ ǻŋ̀hǘ abǫfára nố   They couldn't find the child's
   ŋhốmã̃.   book.

4. Obuéè abǫfára nố nhốmã̃   He opened the child's book.
   nố.

5. Obuéè ɔpốn nố mã̃a mɛ̃.   He opened the door for me.

6. Ǫtǫǫ ɔpốn nố mǘ mã̃a mɛ̃.   He closed the door for me.

7. Ǫtǫǫ kǎà nố mǘ.   He locked the car up.

8. Ná ɔtę kǎà nố mǘ.   He was sitting in the car.

9. Ná ɔtę kyęrɛ́wpốn nⁱ nố.   She was sitting at the desk.

10. Mɛ̃bɛŋ kyęrɛ́wpon nố hố.   I'm near the desk.

Question and Answer Drill A

1. Hwã̃ń na ná wǫ́ nɛ̃ nố   With whom were you talking?
   rękasa nố?
   Ná mɛ̃ nɛ̃ mɛ̃ yę́rę   I was talking to my wife.
   ɛɛkasa.

2. Ná mốokã̃ ɛdę̃ɛ̃ñ hố asɛ́m What where you talking about?
   Ná yɛɛkã̃́ asórę hố   We were talking about
   asɛ́m.   church.

137

3. Ɛdɛɛ́n na ɔ́opɛ?   What did she want?

   Ɔopɛ baabí áà   She wanted to know where she
      yebésɪesìe nɛ̂ káà   could get her car fɪxed.
      amã́ nɔ̃́.

4. Ɛhéfã́ na wɔ́kyɛreɛ̀ nɔ̃́?   Where did you send her?

   Mɛ̃kyɛrɛ̀ɛ̀ nɔ̃́ sɛ́ɛ̀   I told her to go to Kegyetɪa
      ɔ́nkɔ Kégyetɪạ   Crossroad.
      Ŋkwantá.

5. Ɛdɛɛ́n ntí na wɔ́kyɛreɛ̀   Why did you send her there?
   nɔ̃́ sɛ́ɛ̀ ɔ́nkɔ hɔ́?

   Wón nɔ̃́ yɛ́ ạ́dwùma pá   I sent her there because they
      entí na mɛ̃kyɛrɛ̀ɛ̀   do good work.
      nɔ̃́ sɛ́ɛ̀ ɔ́nkɔ hɔ́.

6. Wɔ́ atáádɛɛ̀ nɔ̃́ ạní tɛ   What color are your clothes?
   sɛ̃́ñ?

   Matáádɛɛ yɛ fítaa nɛ̂   My clothes are whɪte and lɪght
      tuntúm kakɛrá.   blue.

7. Mĩ́ñɣạ̃ lɛ́tɛ̀ nné?   Did I get any maɪl today?

   Wúñɣạa lɛ́tɛ̀ baakɔ̃́   You got only one letter.
      pɛ́.

8. Ɔmã́ñ bɛ̃́n mṹ na wúfɪrɪ?   What country are you from?

   Mĩ́fɪrɪ Ghánà mã́ñ mṹ.   I'm from the country of Ghana.

9. Kúro bɛ̃́n mṹ na wúfɪrɪ?   Where are you from? (What town
                                     are you from?)

   Mĩ́fɪrɪ Tɛma kúroṁ.   I'm from the cɪty of Tema.

10. Ɛhɛ́na na ɔ́ɔbɔ ɔpɔ́n nɔ́   Who is knocking at the door?
     ą́kyì?

     Ɔhɔ́hǫ́ǫ na ɔɔbɔ́ ɔpɔ́n   A stranger is knocking at
     nɔ́ ą́kyì.   the door.

New words

tǫ   to lay, put; cast, throw;
                                 apply to, lay on

tǫ...mú   to close, shut, lock

bɛ̨   to be near, approach

asórɛ   church service, devotional
                                 meeting

sɔrɛ́, sɔ̃m   to be careful about; worship,
                                 adore

ɔmã́ñ (pl. a-)   nation, people

ɔhɔ́hǫ́ǫ (pl. a-)   stranger, foreigner, guest

kã́...hɔ́ asɛ́m   to talk about, discuss

5. /hyą́ìn/ and /hyúù/ would probably be spelled as they are in
English. See note 2.

6. /ɛɛ-/ may be prefixed to a verb instead of /re-/ even though
there is a noun subject with the verb. See Question and Answer
Drill A, sentence 1.

7. Certain high tone adjectives compund with nouns and have
similar tone changes, e.g., /bą̀ąbí pápa/ is /bą̀ąbì pápa/.

139

Unit 15

Basic Dialogue

-A-

bóòsǫ   bus

1   Ehéfá na bóòsǫ nó gyɪna?   Where does the bus stop?

-B-

bóòsǫtapǫ   bus stop

2   Bóòsǫtapǫ nó wɔ ñkyɛ́ñ hó.   The bus stop is over there.

-A-

wěí   this, these, that, those

3   Bóòsǫ wěí kó kúrom anáa?   Does this bus go into town?

-B-

4   Dąąbí, wěí na ɛkó kúrom.   No, that one goes into town.

-A-

5   Yɛgyɛ́ áhě?   How much is the fare?

-B-

6   Yɛgyɛ́ sírèṇ dúnsóṇ.   The fare is seventeen shillings.

-A-

tu   to leave, depart

7   Bɛ́rɛ bɛ́n na bóòsǫ nó tú?   When does the bus leave?

-B-

8   Bóòsǫ nó tú nnónnúm.   The bus leaves at five o'clock.

-A-

9   Bɛ́rɛ bɛ́n na bóòsǫ nó bá?   When does the bus arrive?

-B-

10 Bóòsǫ nó bédu nnóŋkǫ́rõ̀ŋ nế   The bus will arrive at nine
    fế.   thirty.

Notes

1. If an English word that ends in a consonant is borrowed into
Twi, it has a vowel after the final consonant. If the consonant
before this vowel is voiceless, the vowel is usually voiceless
unless followed by another vowel, e.g., /bóòsǫtapǫ́/.

2. /w̃eí/ is interchangeable with /eyí/.

3. When there is an emphatic subject marked by a following /na/,
a subject pronoun is prefixed to the verb, e.g., /w̃eí na ɛkó
kuróm/, literally, 'that one, it goes into town'.

4. Transportation schedules use the twenty-four method for
stating arrivals and departures, but for other purposes the first
hour after noon is one o'clock, etc.

Pattern Drill A

1. Ɛhếfế na bóòsǫ gyínabḝa   Where is the bus station?
   nó wo?

2. Ɛhếfế na kḛtḛkḛ́ gyínabḝa   Where is the train station?
   nó wo?

3. Ɛhếfế na ew̃ímhyến   Where is the airport?
   gyínabḝa nó wo?

4. Ɛhếfế na tḛksíì gyínabḝa   Where is the taxi stand?
   nó wo?

5. Ɛhếfế na hyến gyínabḝa   Where is the harbor?
   wo?

141

Pattern Drill B

1. Bɛ́rɛ bɛ́n na kɛ́tɛkɛ́ nɔ́ What time will the train leave?
   bétu.

2. Bɛ́rɛ bɛ́n na ewĭmhyɛ́n What time will the plane arrive?
   nɔ́ bɛ́ba?

3. Bɛ́rɛ bɛ́n na bɔ́ɔsɔ nɔ́ What time will the bus arrive at
   béduru Kumásɛ. Kumasi?

4. Bɛ́rɛ bɛ́n na ewĭmhyɛ́n nɔ́ What time will the plane leave
   bétu fírı Ŋkɛrã́n? from Accra?

5. Bɛ́rɛ bɛ́n na wɔ́kofa What time are you leaving to
   hyɛ́n nɔ́? catch the ship?

New words

okɛ́tɛkɛ́ (pl. n-) hyena; locomotive, train
ɛhyɛ́n (pl. a-) ship, vessel, liner
ewĭmhyɛ́n, ewĭmũhyɛ́n airplane
   (pl. ñ-)
tɛksíì taxi

Lexical Drill A

1. Pénsɛ̀rɛ ní. Here is a pencil.
   This is a pencil.

2. Pénsɛ̀rɛ nɔ́ ní. Here is the pencil.
   This is the pencil.

3. Pénsɛ̀rɛ bí ní. Here is a pencil of some kind.

4. Pénsɛ̀rɛ nɔ́ bí ní. Here is one of the pencils.
   Here are some of the pencils.
   This is the kind of pencil.

5. Pénsɛ̀rɛ yí ní. HERE is the pencil.
   THIS is the pencil.

Question and Answer Drill A

1. Wǫ́dę̀ lórę̀ anǎa kę́tę̀kę̀   Are you taking the bus or the
    na ɛɛkó Kumásę anǎa?   train to Kumasɪ?
    Dą̀ąbí, mɛ̃́dę ewimũhyɛ̃́ɲ   No, I'm going to Kumasɪ by
    na ɛɛkó Kumásę.   plane?

2. Wǫ́bɛyɛ dę́ɛ̃n na wáko   How will you get to the
    ɛ́ɛrpǫ̀rt hó?   airport?
    Madámfǫ́ bí béba abɛfá   A friend of mine is taking
    mɛ̃ ákò ɛ́ɛrpǫ̀rt hó.   me to the airport.

3. Wátò wǫ tę́kę̀tę́ anǎa?   Did you buy your ticket?
    Mɛ̃́tɔɔ mɛ̃ tę́kę̀tę́ wɔ   I bought my ticket at
    Kíñswèɪ nnéra.   Kingsway's yesterday.

4. Bɔ́ɔsǫ bę́ɛ̃n na ɛkó   Which bus goes to the airport?
    ɛ́ɛrpǫ̀rt?
    Bɔ́ɔsǫ wěí na ɛkó   That bus goes to the airport.
    ɛ́ɛrpǫ̀rt.

5. Bɔ́ɔsǫ nó̃ bédɪ mmę́rę̀tę́   How many minutes will the bus
    áhě̃ wɔ há?   stay here?
    Bɔ́ɔsǫ nó̃ bédɪ mmę́rę̀tę́   The bus will stay here for
    dú wɔ há.   ten minutes.

6. Mpę́ɲ áhě̃ na bɔ́ɔsǫ bí   How often does a bus leave
    taá tú fɪrɪ há?   from here?
    Bɔ́ɔsǫ bí tú fɪrɪ há   A bus leaves from here
    doɲhwérèw bíą̀ra.   every hour.

143

7. Aanę bǒòsǫ áà ɛkó Kumásę   Does the bus go to Kuması by
   kɔfá Koforíduą ansá   way of Koforıdua?
   na akó anáa?
   Áąñ, ɛkɔfá Koforíduą   Yes, ıt goes to Kuması· by
   ansá na akó Kumásę.   way of Koforıdua.

8. Ɛľírı há kó Kumásę   How much ıs the fare from here
   yɛgyę́ ahé?   to Kuması?
   Yɛgyę́ pón baakó fírı   The fare from here to Kuması
   há kó Kumásę.   ıs one pound.

9. Wóbetúmı dę wǫ káà nó   Can you take me to the bus
   áfá mɛ̃ ákɔ bǒòs   station ın your car?
   sótehyę̀n?
   Dąąbí, mɛ̃ yę́rę dę wǫ́   No, but my wıfe wıll take
   bɛ́kɔ bǒòs sótehyę̀n   you to the bus station.
   hó.

10. Dá bɛ́n na wǫbɛsáñ ábà?   What day wıll you return?
   Mésáñ ábà Yáwǫ̀da.   I wıll return Thursday.

New words

   lórę̀   lorry, truck, bus, car

   adamfǫ (adámfǫ̇) (pl. n-nóm)   frıend

   ɛ́ɛrpǫ̀rt   aırport

   tę́kętę̇   tıcket

   aanę   a question marker; Is ıt
                                  true /that/ ....

   sótehyę̀n   station

Lexical Drill B

1. Mfoní pıı wɔ fą́sú nɔ́
   hɔ́.

   There are many pictures on
   the wall.

2. Safówá nɔ́ da fą̀m̀ wɔ
   fą́sú nɔ́ hɔ́.

   The key is lying on the floor
   by the wall.

3. Safówá nɔ́ nná ɔpɔ́ŋ áà
   esí mfénsęrę́ nɔ́ hɔ́
   nɔ́ sɔ́.

   The key isn't on the table
   near the window.

4. Mę̃ sę́kán̄ nná ɔpɔ́ŋ áà
   esí mfénsęrę́ nɔ́ hɔ́
   nɔ́ sɔ́.

   My knife isn't on the table
   near the window.

5. Mě sę́kán̄ da ɔpɔ́ŋ áà
   ɛwɔ fą́sú nɔ́ hɔ́ nɔ́
   asę.

   My knife is lying under the
   table next to the wall.

6. Pénsęrę nɔ́ tɔɔ ɔpɔ́ŋ áà
   ɛwɔ fą́sú nɔ́ hɔ́ nɔ́
   asę.

   The pencil fell under the
   table by the window.

7. Pénsęrę nɔ́ tɔɔ adáká
   áà esí ɔpɔ́nɔ̃ nɔ́
   ñkyén̄ nɔ́ mú.

   The pencil fell into the box
   by the table.

8. Mēdę sékán̄ átɔ̀ adáká
   áà esí ɔpɔ́nɔ̃ nɔ́
   ñkyén̄ nɔ́ mú.

   I put the knife into the box
   by the table.

9. Mɛdɛ sékáñ <u>twáá náḿ</u>   I cut the meat with a knife.
   <u>nó mú</u>.

10. Mɛdɛ sékáñ <u>nó áhyɛ̀ mē</u>   I put the knife into my
    <u>kotokú mú</u>.   pocket.

New words

mfoní	picture
pıı	many, much
ɛfá	earth, soil, dirt
efám̀	ground, floor, bottom; below
mfɛ̀ǹsɛ̨rɛ̨́	window
tɔ	to drop, full, **fall**, rain
twą	to cut, cut up; cross, pass by
hyɛ	to stick into, be stuck into; wear, put on (clothes)
kotokú (pl. ŋ-)	pocket, bag

Question and Answer Drill B

1. Wú kúrom̀ kásá yɛ dɛ̨ɛ́ñ?   What is your native language?
   Mí kúrom̀ kásá yɛ   My native language is Twi.
   <u>Twíì</u>.

2. Mmɛ̨́rɛ̨ bɛ̃n na wɔ̨́kɔ   What time do you leave for work?
   ą́dwùma?
   Mɛ̃kɔ́ ą́dwùma <u>nnón</u>   I leave for work at eight
   <u>ŋwɔtwɛ́</u>.   o'clock.

3. Aanɛ̨ wɔ̨́nàntɛ̨́ kó ą́dwùma?   Do you walk to work?
   <u>Sɛ eˇwím̀ yɛ́ áà</u>,   I walk to work when the
   mɛ̃nantɛ̨́ kó ą́dwùma.   weather is nice.

4. Sɛ osúo tó áà, wǫ́dę̨   Do you ride the bus to work
   bóɔ́sǫ na ɛkó ą́dwùma?   when it rains?
   Dąąbí, sɛ osúo tó   No, I drive to work when it
   áà, mę̄ką́ mę̄ ká́à   rains.
   na ɛkó ą́dwùma.

5. Hɛ́na na ɔhwɛ́ mmǫfára   Who looks after the children
   nǒ sǫ́ mmę̨r(ę) áà wǫ   while your wife is working?
   yę́rę ręyɛ́ ą́dwùma?
   Mę̄ yę́rę mą̄amɛ́ na   My wife's mother looks after
      ɛhwɛ́ mmǫfára nǒ sǫ́   the children while my wife
      mmę̨r(e) áà mę̄ yę́rę   works.
      ręyɛ́ ą́dwùma.

6. Ná wǫ́wɔ hǎ nnɔ́ra?   Were you here yesterday?
   Dąąbí, ná mɪnnɪ́ hǎ   No, I wasn't here yesterday.
   nnɛ́ra.

7. Ɛdę̨ɛ̌n na ná wǫ́ǫyɛ   What were you doing when he
   mmę̨r(ę) áà ɔbaayɛ   came?
   nǒ?
   Ná mį̄ɪdɪdɪ́ mmę̨r(ę)   I was eating when he came.
   áà ɔbaayɛ ńo.

8. Obí wo há áà obétùmɪ   Is there anyone here who can
   abǫa mę̄?   help me?
   Sáà mą̄amɛ́ yɪ́ bétùmɪ   That woman can help you.
   abǫa wǫ.

147

9. Wúbetúmı ásǎñ ábà   Can you come back tomorrow?
   ɔkyɛ́ńǎ?

   Métúmı ásǎñ ábà   I can come back tomorrow
   ɔkyɛ́na ow̌ıgýınaɛ́.   afternoon.

10. Sɛ osúo tɔ́ áà, wɔ́bɛkɔ?   If it rains, will you go?
    Ą̌ǎñ, sɛ osúo tɔ́ áà,   Yes, I will go if it rains.
    mɛ́kɔ.

New words

    ew̌ı́m̀   air, atmosphere, weather

Lexical Drill C

1. Mɛ́ba nnónsı̨́ ą́kyı̀.   I will come after six o'clock.

2. Mɛ́ba __wu fíe anądwɔ́__   I will come to your house
   __yı́__.   tonight.

3. __Mǎ yɛŋkɔ́__ wu fíe   Let's go to your house this
   ą̌ñwumɛ́rɛ yı́.   evening.

4. Mǎ yɛŋkɔ́fa bɔ́ɔsɔ ŋkɔ́   Let's go to Kumasi by bus.
   Kumásɛ̨.

5. __Ɛmfá__ bɔ́ɔsɔ ŋkɔ́ Kumásɛ̨. Don't go to Kumasi by bus.

6. Ɛmfá ɔkɛ́ramǎn nɔ́ mmá.   Don't bring the dog.

7. Ɔkɛ́ramǎn nɔ́ mmá __fíe__   The dog doesn't come into the
   __há__.   house.

8. __Mǔ mǔ baakɔ́__ mmá fíe   Don't any of you come into this
   há.   house.

9. Mǔ mǔ baakɔ́ __mmará há__.   One of you come here.

10. __Mǔ mǔ bı́__ mmará há.   Some of you come here.

148

Lexical Drill D

1. Ɔkɔ́ séesei.	He left a short while ago.
2. Ɔkɔ́ <u>séesei áà.</u>	He just left.
3. Mɛ̃ebɛgyɛ́ mɛ́ hɔ́mã <u>síesié áà.</u>	I'm coming over to get my book right away.
4. Mɛ̃ebɛgyɛ́ mɛ́ hɔ́mã <u>séesié.</u>	I'll be over soon to get my book.
5. Mɛ̃ebɛgyé mɛ́ hɔ́mã <u>ɔkyéñã anɔpá.</u>	I'll be over to get my book tomorrow morning.

5. A locomotive is called /ɔkɛ́tɛkɛ̀/, 'hyena', supposedly because it howls like a hyena.

6. /sɔ́tehyɛ̀n/, usually // station//, is often used as frequently as /ɛyínabɛ̀a/.

7. Spatial relationships are indicated by a class of verbs indicating location plus a nominal compound or phrase whose last noun indicates location or part, e.g., /Safówá nɔ́ da ɔpɔ́n nɔ́ sɔ́/, 'The key lies the table's top', i.e., 'The key is on the table'. If a third item or location occurs in a sentence, it is in a subordinate clause with /áà/, e.g., /Safówá nɔ́ da ɔpɔ́ŋ áà esí mfɛ̃nsɛ́rɛ̀ nɔ́ hɔ́ nɔ́ sɔ́/, 'The key lies the table's top which stands the window's exterior', i.e., 'The key is on the table by the window'.

8. Instrumental relationships are shown by /dɛ̀/, 'to have', plus the instrument or tool plus a second verb which shows what is done with the instrument, e.g., /Mɛ̃dɛ̀ sékã́ñ twáą nám nɔ́ mú/, 'I take knife cut the meat's insides', i.e., 'I cut the meat with a knife'.

149

9. Partitive constructions are possessive compounds with /mű/, 'entirety', 'whole', plus a numeral or adjective of quantity, e.g., /mű mű baakő/, 'your entirety's one', i.e., 'one of you'.

10. /séései áà/ is sometimes /séései ára/. /ára/ is 'just', 'even', 'ever', 'the very'.

11. /kő/, 'to go', 'go to', when used as the second verb often translates as 'to'. See Question and Answer Drill A, sentence 8.

Unit 16

Basic Dialogue

-A-

tä́ŋkę	tank
ɛmä́	full
hyɛ...mä́	to fill up
1 Hyɛ mẽ tä́ŋkę nő mä́.	Fill my tank up.

-B-

2 Yǫǫ, matę́.	Yes, I will.
	(Yes, I have understood.)
°ɔ́ę̀lę, ɔ́ę̀yę̀rɛ	oil
3 Wɔ́pè séé mẽhwɛ́ ɔ́ę̀lę nő	Do you want me to check the oil?
anä́a?	

-A-

pa	to take off, skim, scrape
	off; beg, beseech
ɛkyéw	hat, cap
pa kyéw	please
4 Ä́ä̀ñ, mẽpaw kyéw.	Yes, please.

-B-

kɔ́tà	quart
5 ɔ́ę̀lę nő átɔ̀ sĩn béyɛ kɔ́tà	The oil is about a quart low.
baakő.	

151

-A-

gu   to pour; scatter, be
                                         scattered, be located
                                         in groups

Fa baakó gú mú.   Put in one.

°táɛ̀   tire; (necktie)

yíyė   good; repaired, mended

7   Wúbetúmi áyè mẽ táɛ̀ nó yíyė   Can you repair my tire?
    ámã̀ mẽ?

-B-

8   Ã̀ą̃ñ, se wúbetúmi átwèŋ dɛ́   Yes, if you can wait.
    áà.

-A-

gyą   to leave, forsake

ą̀kyíri yí   afterwards

9   Mégyą nő wɔ há na ą̀kyíri yí   I'll leave it here and come for
    mabɛgyɛ́.   it later.

Notes

1. /pa kyɛ́w/ is an idiom which means 'please', or 'I beg you'.
/tu/, 'to pull', 'jerk', 'remove' is used for removing clothing.
/hyɛ/, 'to insert', 'apply to', 'fill' also means 'to put on
clothing'. /pa kyɛ́w/ is used when interupting someone or in
making a request.
    /kɔsɛ/ 'sorry', 'pardon', 'oops', is used when you have
stepped on someone or bumped into someone. /agɔɔ/, besides the
uses given earlier, requests permission to pass, i.e., 'Let me
by', 'Let me through'.

/sɛɾέ/, 'beg', 'ask', is used to make a request of someone, to beg another's pardon or forgiveness, or to interrupt an angered or offended person.

2. After a verb plus /na/, 'and', consecutive forms like /mabɛgyέ/ are sometimes preceeded by a free form, e.g., in sentence 9 of the dialogue /mέba mábègyę̀/ may replace /mabɛgyέ/. Pronouns other than first person singular regularly occur with the consecutive form in this position. Compare Unit 5, note 4.

Lexical Drill A

1. Fa nsúo mã́ gú mĩ́   Fill my cup up with water.
   kúruwà nố mṹ.

2. Hwiè nsúo nố firi   Pour the water out of my cup.
   kúruwà nố mṹ.

3. Hwiè nsúo nố firi   Pour the water out of the
   bǫ́kę̀tę nố mṹ.   bucket.

4. Nsúo nni bǫ́kę̀tę nố   There is no water in the bucket.
   mṹ.

5. Nsúo nni hó áà yɛdę́   There is no water here to wash
   bέhǫ̀rǫ.   with.

6. Sąmínà nni hó áà yɛdę́   There is no soap here to wash
   bέhǫ̀rǫ.   with.

7. Sąmínà nni pố nố nố sǫ́.   There is no soap on the table.

8. Ŋgố nố wɔ pốnố nố sǫ́.   The cooking oil is on the table.

9. Ŋgố nố yɛ mέ mã̃amέ   The palm oil belongs to my
   dę́a.   mother.

10. Kúruwà kę́tęwaa fítaa   The small white cup belongs to
    nố yɛ mέ mã̃amέ dę́ą.   my mother.

153

New words

ekúruwá	cup, pitcher
hwié	to pour out of
bɔ́kɛ̀tɛ̀	bucket
sąmínà (sąmínã̀)	soap
ŋgó	palm oil, cooking oil

Lexical Drill B

1. Ɔkyɛ́nã́ yɛ dá bɛ́n?

What day is tomorrow?

2. Ɔkyɛ́nã́ yɛ Kwą̀siąda.

Tomorrow will be Sunday.

3. Ná Owúsunõm wɔ há
   Kwą̀siąda.

The Owusus were here Sunday.

4. Ná Owúsunõm yɛ
   osukúùfɔ́o w(ɔ)
   Amɛ́rɛ̀ka.

The Owusus were students in
   America.

5. Ná mayɛ́ ą̀dwúma wɔ
   pɛtɛróò dɔ́mpɔ̀ wɔ
   Amɛ́rɛ̀ka.

I worked in a filling station
   in America.

6. Ná mayɛ́ ą̀dwúma
   anwumɛ́rɛ̀ ná makó
   sukúù anɔpá.

I worked at night and I went to
   school during the day.

7. Ná mayɛ́ ą̀dwúma mą́ nó
   ansã́ na mɛ̀baa há.

I had worked for him a year
   before I came here.

8. Yɛhyɛɛ mɛ̃ tą̀ŋkɛ̀ nó mą́
   ansã́ mɛ̀baa há.

I had my tank filled up before
   I came here.

9. Yɛhyεε mɛ̃ táŋkε nő   I had my tank filled up at
    mã́ wɔ Owúsú hɔ́.   Owusu's.

10. Mɛ̃tɔɔ ataadɛ́ɛ yí wɔ   I bought these clothes at
    Owúsú hɔ́.   Owusu's.

New word

    pɛtɛ̨róò dɔ́mpɔ̨   filling station

Lexical Drill C

1. Mɛ̃da asɛ̨.   Thanks.

2. Kyɛ̨rɛ́ asɛ̨.   Translate it.

3. Tɔ́ asɛ̨.   Make a deposit.
                                Pay something down.

4. Tɛ̨rá asɛ̨.   Sit down.

5. Fí asɛ̨.   Start. Begin.

6. Hwɛ̨́ asɛ̨.   Fall down.

7. Hwɛ́ asɛ̨.   Look under it.

8. Bɛ̨rá asɛ̨.   Be humble. Come down off your
                                high horse. Bend over.
                                Stoop down.

9. Dí asɛ̨.   Strike a bargain.
                                Agree on a price.

10. Twá asɛ̨.   Draw a line under it.

Lexical Drill D

1. Waká ąkyírı: He's late.

2. Obedurúù hą́ ąkyírı.   He arrived late.

3. Obedurúù há mmɛ̨́rɛ̨ nő   He arrived on time.
    pɛ́pεεpε.

4. Wąbéduru há mmę́r(ę)   He is on time.   He is in time.
   nɔ́ pɛ́pɛɛpɛ.   He has arrived in time.

5. Wąbéduru há ntɛ́m.   He is on time.

6. Ewimhyɛ́n nɔ́ ąbédu há   The bus arrived on time.
   ntɛ́m.

7. Ewimhyɛ́n nɔ́ ąbédu   The airplane arrived on
   mmę́r(ę) áà yáhyę̀hyɛ́   schedule.
   ámà̃ nɔ́ pɛ́pɛɛpɛ.

8. Bɔ́ɔsǫ nɔ́ bédu mmę́r(ę)   The bus will arrive on schedule.
   áà yáhyę̀hyɛ́ ámà̃ nɔ́
   pɛ́pɛɛpɛ.

9. Bɔ́ɔsǫ nɔ́ béka ąkyíri   The bus will arrive an hour
   dǫnhwę́rę̀ kɔ́.   late.

10. Bɔ́ɔsǫ nɔ́ béduru há   The bus will arrive an hour
    ntɛ́m dǫnhwę́rę̀ kɔ́.   early.

New words

ntɛ́m   haste, swiftness; fast, quick;
                               early, soon

hyę̀hyɛ́   to arrange, adjust; fit out,
                               equip

abáawa (pl. m-)   girl

pę̀rá   to sweep

ądíhǫ, ądíwǫ   yard, court

pę̀rá̀ę̀   broom

156

Lexical Drill E

1. Abáawa nɔ́ rɛpɛ̞rá   The girl is sweeping the yard.
    ądíwo.

2. Abáawa nɔ́ wɔ pɛ̞ráȩ̀   The girl has a new broom.
    fɔ́fɔ̞rǫ.

3. Abáawa nɔ́ dɛ̞́ pɛ̞ráȩ̀   The girl is sweeping with a
    na ɛɛpɛ̞rá.   broom.

4. Abáawa nɔ́ dɛ̞ pɛ̞ráȩ̀   The girl is sweeping with the
    áà mɛ̃yɛ́ máà nõ nɔ́   broom I made for her.
    na ɛɛpɛ̞rá.

5. Abáawa nɔ́ ą́fì asȩ   The girl has begun to sweep the
    pɛ̞rá.   room.

6. Abáawa nɔ́ pɛ̞ráà dą́n   The girl has just swept the
    nɔ́ mű sɩ́ȩsɩe áà.   room.

7. Abáawa nɔ́ apɛ̞rá dą́n   The girl has finished sweeping
    nɔ́ mű ą́w̌ìe.   the room.

8. Abáawa nɔ́ mpɛ̞ráà ɔdą́n   The girl hasn't swept the room
    nɔ́ mű (ɛɛ).   yet.

9. Abáawa nɔ́ mfíì asȩ́   The girl hasn't started to
    mpɛ̞ráà yɛ.   sweep yet.

10. Ą́fèɪ ansą́ na abáawa   The girl is about to sweep now.
    nɔ́ bɛ́pɛ̞ra.

157

Pattern Drill A

1. Sɛ mɪgyá mɛ̃ mpábɔ̀a
   nɛ̃ áà, wúbetùmɪ
   áyɛ̀ ámà̃ mɛ̃ anáã?

   If I leave my shoes, can you
   repair them?

2. Sɛ mɛ̃dɛ mɛ̃ káà nɛ̃
   bá áà, wúbetùmɪ
   áyɛ̀ ámà̃ mɛ̃ anáã?

   If I bring my car can you repair
   it for me?

3. Sa mɛ̃dɛ mɛ̃ káà nɛ̃ bá
   áà, wɔ̃dɛ̀ ɔ̀ɛ̀yɛrɛ
   fɔ̃fɔ̀rɔ̃ bégu mũ ámà̃
   mɛ̃ anáã?

   If I bring my car will you
   change the oil?

4. Sɛ mɛ̃bá ntɛ̃m áà, wɔ̃dɛ̀
   ɔ̀ɛ̀yɛrɛ fɔ̃fɔ̀rɔ̃ bégu
   mũ ámà̃ mɛ̃ anáã?

   If I come early, will you change
   the oil for me?

5. Sɛ mɛ̃bá ntɛ̃m áà ɛsɛ
   sɛ̃ɛ̀ mɛ̃twɛ́n nɛ̃.

   If I call early, I'll have to
   wait for him.

6. Sɛ wammá áà, ɛsɛ sɛ̃ɛ̀
   mɛ̃twɛ́n nɛ̃.

   If he doesn't come, I'll have
   to wait for him.

7. Sɛ wammá áà, yenní
   nàm áà yebédɪ.

   If he doesn't come, we won't
   have any meat to eat.

8. Sɛ yaŋkũm oguã̀ñ áà
   yenní nàm áà yebédɪ.

   If we don't kill a sheep, we
   won't have any meat to eat.

9. Sɛ yaŋkũm oguã̀ñ áà
   ɔkɔ́m bédɛ yɛŋ.

   If we don't kill a sheep, we'll
   be hungry.

10. Sɛ yammá ntɛ̃m áà,
    ɔkɔ́m bédɛ yɛŋ.

    If we don't get back early,
    we'll be hungry.

kũm   to kill, execute; cause
                                 to cease, extinguish

oguáñ   sheep
    |

okóm   hunger

3.   Verbs whose noun objects indicate place or location very
often have meaning which cannot be guessed. See Lexical Drill C.
The student should learn these verbs plus objects as vocabulary
items.

4.   /-wa/, /-ma/, /-ba/ are productive suffixes, i.e., are used
to form many new words. /-wa/ means 'feminine' or 'the female'
of the noun to which it is attached. If /-wa/ is preceeded by
a single /-a/, /-awa/ is usually /-aá/, e.g., /Atá/, 'a male twin',
and /Ataá/, 'a female twin'. /-ma/ means the 'masculine' or 'the
male' of the noun. /-ba/ means, 'the child of' or 'the young of'
the noun.

5.   A low-tone /-ẹ/ suffix forms instrument nouns from verbs,
e.g., /pẹráẹ̀/, 'broom' from /pẹrá/, 'to sweep' and /fitáẹ̀/,
'bellows', 'a woven fan', from /fitá/, 'to fan a fire'. Though
this suffix is fairly common, the student should avoid coining
new verb stems.

6.   /ná/ plus the perfect makes up the past perfect. See Lexical
Drill B, sentences 6 and 7.

159

Unit 17

Basic Dialogue

-A-

1 Mɛ̃paw kyɛ́w.   I beg your pardon.

    edwómũ (pl. (e)ññw̃ómũ)   market, market place

2 Ɛhɛ́fá na edwómũ wɔ?   Where is the market?

-B-

    tɛ̃e   straight

3 Kó wąnim̀ tɛ̃e.   Go straight. ('Go your face-
                                plane straight.')

    nıfá̃ (nífã)   right

4 Sɛ wų́duru sukúùdáñ nɔ́ hɔ́   When you reach the school, turn
    áà, fa wų́ nífã.   right.

     bɛ̃ŋkũ̀m (bɛ̃nkũm)   left

     ɔhɛ́ṇ (hɛ́ṇ)   king, chief

      (pl. a-nŏm)

5 Fa wɔ bɛ̃nkũ̃m wɔ Ɔhɛ́ṇ   Turn left at King's Junction.
    Ŋ̀kwantá.

     kɔ sɔ́   to keep on, continue

6 Kɔ sɔ́ kɔ tɛ̃e kosí sɛ́ɛ̀   Keep on going until you come
    wų́bedu edwómũ nɔ́ hɔ́.   to the market.

-A-

7 Mmɛ́rẹ sɛ̃n na métùmı dẹ   How long will it take me to
    ánàntẹ ą́dùru hɔ́?   walk there?

- B-

dę   to take, require

8 Wúbetúmı dę doŋhwę́rę́fã   It wıll take you half an hour
   ą́dùru.   to get there.

Notes

1. /guą́ą́sǫ/, whıch ıs // guaso//, ıs also commonly used for 'market'
'market'. Thıs ıs an Akuapım word meanıng 'an assembly', 'place
where people come together', 'market'.

2. /dę/ also ıs used ın the sense of 'takıng or requırıng a
certaın amount of tıme or a certaın tool (ıncludıng money) to do
a certaın actıvıty'.

Question and Answer Drıll A

1. Ɔlıwã́ñ bɛ́n na ɛkó   Whıch road goes to the market?
    edwómũ?

    Ɔlıwã́ñ áà ɛdą́ nıfã́   The road on the rıght goes
    nɔ̃́ kó edwómũ.   to the market.

2. Guą́ą́sǫkwã́ñ wɔ hɛ́?   Where ıs the market road?
    Guą́ą́sǫkwã́ñ wɔ   The market road ıs on the
    bẽnkṹm.   left.

3. Ɛhɛ́fã́ na bóòsǫgyınábę́a   Where ıs the bus station?
    nɔ̃́ wɔ?
    Bóòsǫgyınábę̀a nɔ̃́ wɔ   The bus station ıs /straıght/
    wąním̀.   ahead.

4. Ɔkwã́ñ yí kó hɛ́?   Where does thıs road go?
    Ɔkwã́ñ yí kó mpǫanɔ̃́.   Thıs road goes to the seasıde.

161

5. Ɛhɛfá na lórɛ̀ nő fáày?   Which way did the car go?

    Lórɛ̀ nő <u>fáà</u> bĕnkŭm.   The car took a left.

6. Ɛdɛɛ̨́n na ɛbó wɔ nsá   What are you wearing on your

    bĕnkŭm nő?   left arm?

    <u>Wákyɛ̀</u> na ɛbó mĕ nsá   I'm wearing a watch on my

    bĕnkŭm nő.   left arm.

7. Wɔ́yɛ̀ɛ dɛɛ̨́n na wútwạá   How did you cut your right

    wɔ nsá nɪfá?   hand?

    <u>Sékáń</u> na etwáạ̀ mĕ   It was a knife that cut my

    nsá nɪfá.   hand.

8. Dá bĕn na yedí guạ?   What day is the market held?

    Yedí guạ <u>Bɛnada</u>.   Market day is Tuesday.

9. Ɔfaa kwáń w̌eí sɔ́ anáa   Did he take this road or that

    sɛ́ɛ̀ w̌eí sɔ́?   one?

    Ɔfaa kwáń <u>w̌eí sɔ́</u>.   He took this road.

10. Yɛbɛ́tɔ̨a sɔ́ ákɔ̀ yɛŋ   Shall we continue on straight

    ạním tĕe anáa?   ahead?

    <u>Dạạbí</u>, yɛntɔ̨á sɔ́   No, we aren't going to

    ákɔ̀ yɛŋ ạním tĕe?   continue on straight ahead.

New words

ɛpɔ	ocean, sea
anő	mouth; edge, brim; beginning
mpɔanő, ɛpɔanő	seaside, seashore
bɔ	to tie, tie up, tie on
wákyɛ̀	watch
tɔ̨á	to join, connect, string; follow, continue

162

Lexical Drill A

1. Mẽdę ṣąmína na ɛhǫ́rǫ̀ǫ̀   I used soap to wash my car.
   mẽ káà nố.

2. Mẽdę ṣąmína hǫ́rǫ̀ǫ̀ mẽ   I washed my car with soap.
   káà nố.

3. Mẽtɔnn mẽ káà nố.   I sold my car.

4. Mẽtɔnn bayę́rɛ wɔ   I sold yams at the market.
   edwómũ.

5. Mĩhũu bayę́rɛ wɔ   I saw yams at the market.
   edwómũ.

6. Mĩhũu nố sɛ́ɛ́ óohǫrǫ   I saw him washing his car.
   ñe káà nố.

7. Mẽgyę́ mĩdí sɛ́ɛ́ óohǫrǫ   I believe he is washing his car.
   ñe káà nố.

8. Mẽgyę́ mĩdí sɛ́ɛ́ osúo   I believe it will rain today.
   bɛ́tɔ nnɛ́.

9. Obisáà mẽ sɛ́ɛ́ osúo   He asked me if it will rain
   bɛ́tɔ nnɛ́.   today.

10. Obisáà mẽ nęa eguą́ą́sǫ   He asked me where the market
    wɔ?   is?

New words

   gyę́ dí   to believe

   bayę́rɛ   yam

163

Question and Answer Drill B

1. Ɛdɛɛ́n ntí na wúusą́ń   Why are you going back to school
   ákɔ sukúù mú bío?   again?
      Mɪ̀ɪsą́ń ákɔ sukúù mú   I'm going back to school
      bío ésīanǫ sɛ́ɛ́   because I forgot my coat.
      mẽw̃ǫrɛ áfìrɪ mɛ́
      kóòt.

2. Mpɛ́ɲ ahɛ́ na mɔ́tǫ ábà?   How often do you hold elections?
      Yɛtǫ́ ábà mfíe nứm   We hold elections every five
      bíara.   years.

3. Ɛkwɑ́ɲ yí kɔ́ hé?   Where does this road go?
      Ɛkwɑ́ɲ yí kɔ́ ąkuraá   It goes down to a certain
      bí asǫ.   village.

4. Ɛdɛɛ́n ntí na wámma.   Why didn't you come last Friday?
      Fíeda áà etwą́ mú nɔ́?
      Mammá Fíeda áà etwą́   I didn't come last Friday
      mú nɔ́ efɪ sɛ́ɛ́ mɛ̃   because my wife went on a
      yǫ́rǫ ątù kwɑ́ɲ.   trip.

5. Wɔ́ nɛ̃ mɛ̃ bɛ́ko Mǫ́mǫnęda   Are you going to go with me
   áà ɛ́ɛba yɪ?   next Saturday?
      Mɛ́èntumí nɛ̃ wɔ́ ŋkɔ́   I won't be able to go with
      Mǫ́mǫnęda áà ɛ́ɛba   you next Saturday.
      yɪ.

6. Póstòfès nó wo wạním   Is the post office straight
   anáa?   ahead?
   Dąạbí, póstòfès nó   No, the post office ıs back
   wɔ w(o) ákyì.   that way.

7. Ɛdeɛ́n na wóyɛɛ̀ mmẹ́r(e)   What did you do after I left?
   áà mıfíì há nó?
   Mmẹ́r(e) áà wúfıì há   I went to look around the
   nó, mɛ̃kohwɛɛ̀   House of Parliament.
   Omáñ̃ñ̃hyıàmúdáñ̃.

8. Wákòhwɛ́ Asantẹhẹ́nẹfıe   Have you ever seen the
   pɛŋ anáa?   Ashantıhene's palace?
   Áañ̃, mɛ̃kɔɔ hó sɛ́ɛ̀   Yes, I went there especıally
   mɛ̃ekohwɛ́   to see the Ashantıhene's
   Asantẹhẹ́nẹfıe.   palace.

9. Wọ́kɔɔ̀ ahọ́mfıe nó,   When you went to the palace,
   wúhṹu Sıkáągùạ   did you see the Golden Stool?
   Kofí nó anáa?
   Dąạbí, mañ̃ñ̃yạ́ kwá̃n   No, I didn't have an oppor-
   áṇkohwɛ́ Sıkáągùạ   nıty to see the Golden Stool.
   Kofí nó.

10. Wúhṹu Asantẹhẹ́nẹ   Did you see the Asantehene
    áṇkasa?   himself?
    Dąạbí maṇhṹ nó;   No, I didn't see him; but
    mmɔ̃m mĩhṹu nɛ̃   rather I talked to his
    kyéáme.   spokesman.

165

New words

w̌ẹ́rɛ̀	mind, memory; the seat of the emotions
w̌ẹ́rɛ̀ fɪ(rɪ)	to forget
tọ ba	to elect, choose
ạkuraá asẹ	village
okurạạsénì (pl. ŋ-fọ́o)	villager
tu kwáñ	to travel, take a trip
Ɔmáññhyɪạmúdáñ	House of Parliament
Asantẹ́	Ashanti language or region
Asantẹhẹ́nẹ	the King of Ashanti
pɛŋ	before, previously
ahẹ́mfɪe	palace, chief's house
Sɪkạ́ạgùạ Kofí	the Golden Stool
ñyạ́ kwáñ	to have an opportunity, get the chance
áŋkasa	self
ḿmɔ̌ḿ	rather
okyẹ́ámẹ (pl. a-)	a chief's spokesman

Pattern Drill A

1. Ná mẹ̃yɛ́ abọfára nɔ́,
   mẽtẹráà Ŋkẹráñ.

   When I was a child, I lived in Accra.

2. <u>Mmẹ́r(ẹ) áà mẽwɔ Ghánà</u>
   <u>nɔ́</u>, mẽtẹnáà Ŋkẹráñ.

   While I was in Ghana, I stayed in Accra. When I was in Ghana, I lived in Accra for a while.

166

3. Mmę́r(ę) áà mẽwɔ Ghánà   When I was ın Ghana, I lıved
   nɔ́, ná mẽtę Ŋkę̣rạ̈́ñ.   ın Accra.

4. Mẽ́ papá w̌úì nɔ́, ná   When my father dıed, I lıved
   mẽtę Ŋkę̣ rạ̈́ñ.   ın Accra.

5. Mẽ́ papá w̌úì nɔ́, ná   When my father dıed, I was ten
   mą̣dí mfíe dú.   years old.

6. Mmę́r(ę) áà yetú kɔ́ɔ̀   When we moved to Takoradı, I
   Tạ̈kòrą̣dı, ná mą̣dí   was ten years old.
   mfíe dú.

7. Mmę́r(ę) áà yetú kɔ́ɔ̀   When we moved to Takoradı, my
   Tạ̈kòrą̣dı, ná yɛŋwɔ̣́ɔ̣   sıster wasn't born yet.
   mî ñúabàa nɔ́ ɛɛ.

8. Mmę́r(ę) áà mîfíì sukúù   When I started to school, my
   ᴀꜱę̣ nɔ́, ná yɛŋwɔ̣́ɔ̣   sıster wasn't born yet.
   mî ñúạbàa nɔ́ ɛɛ.

9. Mmę́r(ę) áà mîfíì sukúù   When I started to school, we
   asę́ nɔ́, ná yɛtę   lıved close to the school.
   sukúùdä́ñ nɔ́ ñkyę́ñ
   pɛɛ.

10. Ná mẽ̀yɛ́ abǫfára nɔ́,   When I was a chıld, we lıved
    ná yɛtę sukúùdä́ñ   close to the school.
    nɔ́ ñkyę́ñ pɛɛ.

167

Lexical Drill B

1. Ɔpoŋkó nő da ɔkwắn
   nő mú.

   The horse is lying in the road.

2. Ɔpoŋkó nő gyina ɔkwắn
   nő mú.

   The horse is standing in the road.

3. Mpoŋkó nő bɔa ɔkwắn
   nő mú.

   The horses are lying together in the street.

4. Mpoŋkó nő bɔábɔ̀a ɔkwắn
   nő mú.

   The horses are lying about in groups in the street.

5. Mpoŋkó nő dẹda ɔkwắn
   nő mú.

   The horses lying about in the road.

6. Mpoŋkó nő gyinạgyina
   ɔkwắn nő mú.

   The horses are standing about in the street.

Lexical Drill C

1. Duá̀ da fắm̀.

   There is a stick lying on the floor.

2. Nnuá̀ gu fắm̀.

   There are trees lying on the ground.

3. Nnuá̀ gugu fắm̀.

   There are sticks scattered on the ground.

4. Nnuá̀ dẹda fắm̀.

   There are logs lying about the ground.

5. Nnuá̀ sisi fắm̀.

   There are trees /standing/ about the ground.

New words

ɔpɔŋkó (póŋkɔ) (pl. m-)	horse
bɔa	to lie or lay in a group
dué (nnué)	tree, stick, wood

Lexical Drill D

1. Ɔkǒm dę mɛ̃.   I'm hungry. ('Hunger possesses me.')

2. Osukǒm dę mɛ̃.   I'm thirsty.

3. Awó dę mɛ̃.   I'm cold.

4. Ąhúhurɔ dę mɛ̃.   I'm hot.

---

5. Mąní kǔm.   I'm sleepy. ('My eyes are dead.')

6. Mabérɛ.   I'm tired. ('I have /become/ fatigued.')

---

7. Ɛyɛ́ mɛ̃ dɛ.   It's sweet. ('It is /to/ me sweet.')

8. Ɛyɛ́ mɛ̃ ñwęnę.   It's bitter.

9. Ɛyɛ́ mɛ̃ ñkyęnęñkyénę.   It's salty.

---

10. Ewǐm yɛ hyę.   It's hot. ('The air is hot.')

11. Ewǐm yɛ ñwǐnì.   It's cold.

169

New words

ɔkóm	hunger
awɔ́	cold, chill
ạhúhurǫ	heat, steam
kũm	to die, be dead, kill
bęrɛ	to fatigue, grow weary
dɛ	sweet; pleasant, agreeable
ñw̃ęnę	bitter, sour
ñkyɛ́nę	salt
ñkyęnęñkyę́nę	salty
hyę	to burn; hot
ñw̌ínĩ	cool

3. /mẽw̃ę́rè ạ́fìrı/ is often /mĩw̃í ạ́fìrı/.

4. Before the Europeans came the Ashanti Empire controlled most of the central and southern part of what is now Ghana. The /Asantęhę́nę/ or King of the Ashanti ruled from Kumasi where he sat on the Golden Stool, which was believed to have descended from heaven. One did not directly address a chief, but one spoke to the king's /okyę́ãmę/, 'spokesman', who whispered the message to the chief. The spokesman then gave the king's reply to the inquirer.

5. /áŋkasa/ may be preceeded by independent personal pronouns, e.g., /mẽ áŋkasa/, 'myself'.

6. Most stative verbs showing location are reduplicated to indicate the subjects of the verb are scattered or distributed about in the position or manner indicated by the verb stem.

7. The perfect of some verbs is often used to describe a present
condition resulting from something past, e.g., /mabɛ́rɛ/, 'I'm
tired', literally 'I have /become/ fatigued'.

8. Some adjectives occur only after a verb, e.g., /dɛ/, 'sweet'.
If the verb of the sentence is not a stative verb, this type of
adjective follows the noun in a subordinate clause beginning
with /áà yɛ̂/, 'which is'.

9. /póstòfɛ̝s/ is //posuɔfese//.

Unit 18

Basic Dialogue

-A-

1　Wóyɛ dɛ̀ɛ́ñ ą́dwùma?　　　　　What's your occupation?

-B-

　　kookóò　　　　　　　　　cocoa, cocoa tree
　　ąfúo, ąfúw (pl. m-)　　　　farm, field
　　dɔ　　　　　　　　　　to produce, raise, increase

2　Mĕdɔ́ kookóò ąfúo.　　　　　I'm a cocoa farmer.

-A-

　　sɔ̃́　　　　　　　　　　to be big, be large

3　Wǫ́ ąfúo nɔ̃́ sɔ̃́ anǎa?　　　Is your farm large?

-B-

4　Ą̀ą̀ñ, ɛsɔ̃́ kakęráa.　　　　Yes it's not so big.

-A-

　　yarɛ̨́ɛ (yárɛ̨ɛ) (pl. ñ-)　　sickness, disease

5　Wǫ́ ąfúo nɔ̃́ kookóò yarɛ̨́ɛ wɔ　Are you troubled by swollen
　　mǘ?　　　　　　　　　　shoot disease?

-B-

6　Ą̀ą̀ñ, kookóò yarɛ̨́ɛ ą́kừm nnuą́　Yes, swollen shoot has killed
　　nɔ̃́ fǎ.　　　　　　　　about half my trees.

-A-

7　Entí nnuą́ áà yarɛ̨́ɛ wɔ mǘ　What do you do then with the
　　nɔ̃́ wóyɛ nɔ̃́ dɛ̨̀ɛ́ñ?　　　infected trees?

172

- B-

mmará (mmárá)	law, rule
twą...gu	to cut in various locations
8 Abán mmará kyęrέ sέέ εsε	Government regulations say that
sέέ yetwą́ nnuą́ áà yarę́ε	all infected trees must be cut
wɔ mű nő ñyĭnáa gu.	out.

Notes

1. /εső kakęráa/, 'It's not so big', literally 'It's big a little' is a modest way of implying 'It's quite large'.

2. /kookôò yarę́ε/, 'swollen shoot disease' attacks and kills cocoa trees. At present there is no known cure for swollen shoot. The government pays farmers to cut out infected trees. Ghana is the world's leading producer of cocoa and depends on her export of about a quarter of a million tons per annum for most of her foreign exchange.

3. /Entí...wǫ́yε nő dę́έñ?/ is quite emphatic and shows surprise or other emotion. If emphasis were not desired, dialogue sentence 7 would probably be /Ɛdę́έn na wǫ́dę̀ nnuą́ áà yarę́έ wɔ mű nő yéʔ/, 'What do you do with the infected trees?'.

4. /gu/, 'to be poured, sprinkled, or spread about', is used after another verb to show that the action is performed at various places, or with a number of items, e.g., /twą...gu/, 'to cut out pieces here and there', 'cut at several locations'. Sometimes /gu/ translates 'onto', 'upon'; 'away', e.g., /mētɔɔ pέnsę̀rę nő gúùyε/, 'I threw the pencils away' or /Mētɔɔ pέnsę̀rę nő guu pőŋ sǫ́/, 'I threw the pencils onto the table'.

173

Lexical Drill A

1. Mɛ̃dó kookóò ạfúo wɔ   I'm a cocoa farmer at Juaso.
   Juạ̃ạsọ.

2. Mɛ̃dó ŋkátɛ̣̃ɛ afúo wɔ   I'm a peanut farmer at Mpraeso.
   Mpráẹsọ.

3. Mɛ̃ papá yɛ porísìnì   My father is a policeman at
   wɔ Mpráẹsọ.   Mpraeso.

4. Mɛ̃ papá dì porósì wɔ   My father is in the police at
   Yeńdì.   Yendì.

5. Wɔyɛ́ŋ ạnạntwíe wɔ   They raise cattle at Yendì.
   Yeńdì.

6. Wɔyɛ́ŋ ạnạtwíe wɔ   They raise cattle in Northern
   Esíremũ.   Ghana.

7. Yɛyɛ́ abãñ ạ́dwùma wɔ   We work for the government in
   Esíremũ.   Northern Ghana.

8. Yɛyɛ́ abãñ ạ́dwùma wɔ   We work for the government at
   Adã́a.   Ada.

9. Otú ñkyɛ́nẹ wɔ Adã́a.   He mines salt at Ada.

10. Otú sìká wɔ Obuạ́sì.   He mines gold at Obuasì.

New words

ŋkátɛ̣̃ɛ   peanut, groundnut

porísìnì (pl. m- ~ a- fɔ̣́ɔ)   policeman

pórìsì   police

dì   to work as, be employed as

yɛŋ   to breed, nurse, raise
                                 animals

nąntwíe (nąntwıe)   a head of cattle
  (pl. ąnąntwíe)

ɛsə́rɛ̀ (sérɛ̀)   grass

Esíremũ   the grasslands ın the north
                                     of Ghana

Esıremũfʠɔ   the ınhabıtants of the
                                     grasslands

tú   to dıg, farm, mıne

Lexıcal Drıll B

1. Anõmãá nṍ sı duą́ nṍ sʠ́.   The bırd ıs ın the tree.

2. Anõmãá nṍ ątú ą́kòsı duą́   The bırd has flown ınto the
     nṍ sʠ́.   tree.

3. Anõmãá nṍ ątú ą́fìrı duą́   The bırd has flown out of
     nṍ sʠ́.   the tree.

4. Anõmą́ą́ nṍ ątú ą́fà duą́   The bırd flew under the tree.
     nṍ asę̀.

5. Anõmãá nṍ eetú áfà duą́   The bırd ıs flyıng past the
     nṍ hṍ.   tree.

6. Anõmãá nṍ ątú twą duą́   The bırd flew around the
     nṍ hṍ ą́hyìą̀.   tree.

7. Anõmãá nṍ ątú ko duá   The bırd flew toward the
     nṍ hṍ.   tree.

8. Anõmãá nṍ ątú ą́fìrı   The bırd flew away from the
     duą́ nṍ hṍ.   tree.

9. Anɔ̃mãá nɔ̃́ ą̃tú áfà duą̃
   nɔ̃́ sɔ̃́.

The bird flew over the tree.

10. Anɔ̃mãá nɔ̃́ ą̃tú áfà
    nnuą̃ nɔ̃́ ntɛ́m.

The bird flew between the trees.

New words

anɔ̃mãá (ánɔ̃mãa) (pl. n-)   bird

tu   to fly

ñhyıą̃   meeting, interview, session

Lexical Drill C

1. Ooduą̃ kookóò wɔ náfɔɔ̀m.

He is planting cocoa on his farm.

2. Ooduą̃ kookóò wɔ nnuą̃
   kɛsɛ́ɛ nɔ̃́ asę̣

He is planting cocoa under the tall trees.

3. Nĩ́ fíe sı nnuą̃ kę̣sɛ́ɛ
   nɔ̃́ asę̣.

His house is under the big trees.

4. Nĩ́ fíe sı nsúo nɔ̃́ hɔ̃́.

His house is by the river.

5. Ɔɔnam nsúo nɔ̃́ hɔ̃́.

He is walking by the river.

6. Ɔɔnam nsúoą̣nɔ̀.

He is walking along the river bank.

7. Ɔsáñ kɔɔ nsúoą̣nɔ̀.

He went back to the edge of the river.

8. Ɔsáñ kəfáà nnéɛmã áà
   ná wáḡyą̣ nẽ hó nɔ̃́.

He went down to get the things he had left.

176

9. Ɔkɔɔ sɔ́rɔ̀ hó kofáà   He went up to get his things
    nnɛ̧ɛmã́ áà ná wɛ̧́gyɛ̧   that he had left.
    nɛ̃ hó nɔ̂.
10. Ɔkɔɔ sɔ́rɔ̀ kɔdáày.   I went upstairs and went to
                                bed.

New words

    sã́ñ, sã́nɛ̂   to return
    nsúoa̧nɔ̂   edge of water, riverbank,
                                lakeside
    ɔsɔ́rɔ̀   top, upper part; above, over

Pattern Drill A

1. °Abarȩmáá áà óokasa nɔ̂   The boy who is talking is my
    yɛ mɪ́ ñúa̧.   brother.

2. Abarȩmáá áà óokɔ nɔ̂ yɛ   The boy who is going is my
    mɪ́ ñúa̧.   brother.

3. Abarȩmáá áà óopȩra nɔ̂   The boy who is sweeping is my
    yɛ mɪ́ ñúa̧.   brother.

4. Abarȩmáá áà otȩ́ há nɔ̂   The boy who is sitting there
    yɛ mɪ́ ñúa̧.   is my brother.

5. Abarȩmáá áà opȩrá nɔ̂ yɛ   The boy who sweeps is my
    mɪ́ ñúa̧.   brother.

6. Abarȩmáá áà okó nɔ̂ yɛ   The boy who goes is my
    ·· mɪ́ ñúa̧.   brother.

7. Abarȩmáá áà obɪsá nɔ̂   The boy who asks is my
    yɛ mɪ́ ñúa̧.   brother.

177

8. Abarɛmáá áà ɔtɛ́nãá hó   The boy who sat there is my
    nó yɛ mí ñúą.   brother.

9. Abarɛmáá áà ɔpɛ́raá nó   The boy who swept is my
    yɛ mí ñúą.   brother.

10. Abarɛmáá áà ɔkásaáy nó   The boy who talked is my
     yɛ mí ñúą.   brother.

11. Abarɛmáá áà obísaáy nó   The boy who asked is my
     yɛ mí ñúą.   brother.

12. Abarɛmáá áà ɔbááy nó yɛ   The boy who came is my
     mí ñúą.   brother.

13. Abarɛmáá áà ɔtóóy nó yɛ   The boy who bought it is my
     mí ñúą.   brother.

Pattern Drill B

1. Abarɛmáá áà ɔɔŋkása   The boy who isn't talking is
    nó yɛ mí ñúą.   my brother.

2. Abarɛmáá áà ɔɔŋkó nó   The boy who isn't going is my
    yɛ mí ñúą.   brother.

3. Abarɛmáá áà ɔɔmpɛra nó   The boy who isn't sweeping is
    yɛ mí ñúą.   my brother.

4. Abarɛmáá áà ɔ́ntɛ́ há nó   The boy who isn't sitting
    yɛ mí ñúą.   here is my brother.

5. Abarɛmáá áà ɔ́mpɛra nó   The boy who doesn't sweep is
    yɛ mí ñúą.   my brother.

6. Abarɛmáá áà ɔ́ŋkó nó yɛ   The boy who doesn't go is
    mí ñúą.   my brother.

7. Abaręmáá áà ómmisa nó
   yɛ mí ñúą.

The boy who doesn't ask is
my brother.

8. Abaręmáá áà óntę há nó
   yɛ mí ñúą.

The boy who doesn't sit here
is my brother.

9. Abaręmáá áà wámpęra nó
   yɛ mí ñúą.

The boy who didn't sweep is
my brother.

10. Abaręmáá áà wáŋkása nó
    yɛ mí ñúą.

The boy who didn't talk is my
brother.

11. Abaręmáá áà wómmisa nó
    yɛ mí ñúą.

The boy who didn't ask is my
brother.

12. Abaręmáá áà wámmá nó yɛ
    mí ñúą.

The boy who didn't come is
my brother.

13. Abaręmáá áà wántó nó yɛ
    mí ñúą.

The boy who didn't buy it is
my brother.

New word

abaręmáá (pl. m-)   boy, lad

Lexical Drill D

1. Abáñ áhyęhyɛ mmára
   fófóro pii.

The government has passed
many new laws.

2. Abáñ áhyęhyɛ má
   sukúúfóo ábà Amęręka.

The government has arranged
for students to come to
America.

3. Wabóa má sukúúfóo ábà
   Amęręka.

He has helped students come
to America.

179

4. Waboa me̱ ma̱ máhyȩhyɛ́   He has helped me repair my
   me̱ báȩsȩkȩrɛ.   bicycle.

5. Wóbetúmı ábo̱a me̱ ma̱   Can you help me fix my
   máhyȩhyɛ́ me̱ báȩsȩkȩrɛ.   bicycle?

6. Wóbetúmı ábo̱a me̱ ma̱   Can you help me find Nkrumah
   máhwȩhwɛ́ °Nkúruma   Avenue?
   °A̱vènu?

7. Me̱tȩ Ŋkúruma A̱venu.   I live on Nkrumah Avenue.

8. Me̱tȩ °Kȩmbɛ́rȩ A̱vènu   I live at Kimberly Avenue
   ne̱ °Pégèn °Róòdo   and Pagan Road.
   ŋkwantá.

9. Márko̱la nóma̱ wàn sı   Markola Number One is at the
   Kȩmbɛ́lȩ A̱venu ne̱   corner of Kimberly Avenue
   Pégèn Róòdo̱ ŋkwantá.   and Pagan Road.

10. Márko̱la nóma̱ wàn dí   Markola Number One is next
    Mma̱ra Súkuù só̱.   to the Law School.

New words

        báȩsȩkȩrɛ   bicycle

        dí...só̱   to follow, come after,
                                     be next, to be beside

5. The tone pattern which a verb has in isolation is the primary
tone pattern. The verb in most independent clauses has the primary
pattern. In relative clauses and after emphatic /na/, most verbs
have a different or secondary tone pattern, but the positive simple
present and the positive stative verbs do not have a secondary
pattern. Verb forms that have secondary tone patterns are: (1)
positive progressive and positive perfect, high throughout, (2)

positive past, primary prefixes, high stem vowels, mid tense suffix, high adverbial suffixes, (3) positive future and all negatives, high prefixes, mid on first stem vowel, high on succeeding stem vowels.

6.   /abaręmáà/ is //abarımaa//.

7.   /Ŋkúruma Ávenu/ is /Nkrumah Avenue//.
     /Kęmbęrę̀/ or /Kęmbę́lę̀ Róòdo/ is //Kımberly Road/.
     /Pégę̀n Róòdo/ is //Pagan Road//.

Unit 19

Basic Dialogue

-A-

1 Wúgyı dí séɛ́ osú béto ɛnnɛ́ anáa?   Do you think it will rain today?

-B-

2 Dąąbí, mĩññyí nní séɛ́ osú béto.   No, I don't believe it will rain today.

3 Wǫ́ǫkɔ bąąbí anáa?   Are you going somewhere?

-A-

fǫ́tbɔɔl   soccer

4 Áąñ, mẽpɛ séɛ́ mẽkɔhwé fǫ́tbɔɔl.   Yes, I want to go to a soccer game.

-B-

bóɔl   ball

5 Hwánnõm na ɛɛbó bóɔl ɛnnɛ́?   Which teams are playing today?

-A-

kɔtɔkɔ   brave companions, able teammates

6 Kɔtɔkɔ nɛ̃ °Gerét Ashántę̀s.   The Kotokos and the Great Ashantis.

-B-

7 Sɛ nsúo t(ɔ́) áà, wǫ́bɛyɛ dę̀ɛ́ñ?   What will you do if it rains?

-A-

8 Sɛ nsúo t(ɔ́) áà, métɛ̃nã̄ fíe   If it rains, I'll stay home
   makɛ̃nkã̄ñ mɛ̃́ hɔ́mã̄.   and read.

Notes

1. /-nõm/, which forms the plural of many nouns referring to persons, may also mean 'and those with the subject', e.g., /Owúsunõm/, may mean 'The Owusus (any two or more persons with this name)' or 'Owusu and the people with him'.

Pattern Drill A

1. Wúgyɪ dí sɛ́ɛ̀ ɔɔba?   Do you think he is coming?

2. Wúgyɪ dí sɛ́ɛ̀ ɔɔkɔ?   Do you think he is going?

3. Wúnĩm ɔbarɛ̃má áà ɔoko   Do you know the man who is
    nõ̃?   going?

4. Wúnĩm bɨɨbí áà owoʼ   Do you know where he is?

5. Mĩnnĩm bɑ̨ɑ̨bí áà owɔ.   I don't know where he is.

6. Mĩnnĩm nɛ̨a ɔoyɛ̃.   I don't know what he is doing.

7. Kohwɛ́ nɛ̨a ɔoyɛ.   Go see what he is doing.

8. Kohwɛ́ sɛ́ɛ̀ nsúo ɛɛtɔ.   Go see if it is raining.

9. Bɪsa nõ̃ sɛ́ɛ̀ nsúo ɛɛtɔ.   Ask him if it is raining.

10. Bɪsa nõ̃ sɛ́ɛ̀ Kotokɔ ɛɛbɔ   Ask him if the Kotokos are
    ɛnnɛ́.   playing today.

183

Question and Answer Drill A

1. Tíìm bɛ́n na wɔ́pɛ̀ woŋ
   ásɛ̀m?

   Mɛ̄pɛ Kotoko asɛ́m.   I like the Kotokos.

                           What is your favorite team?

2. Wɔ́gyɛ nɛa ɔká̄aɣɛ nɔ̄
   dí?   Do you believe what he said?

   Dą̄ą̄bí, mañ́ñ́yɛ̨ nɛa   No, I didn't believe what he
   ɔká̄aɣɛ nɔ̄ ą̄nní.   said.

3. Sɛ osúo t(ɔ́) á̀à,   What will you do if it rains?
   wɔ́bɛyɛ dɛ̨ɛ́ñ?

   Sɛ osúo t(ɔ) á̀à,   If it rains, I'm not going to
   mɛ́èŋkó.   go.

4. Mmarɛ̨má nɔ̄ mų̄ nɛa ɔwɔ   Which one of the men is looking
   hɛ̨́n na ɔɔhwɛhwɛ́ mɛ̃?   for me?

   Barɛ̨má á̀à ɔ́ohyɛ   The man wearing the blue
   ataadɛ̨́ɛ ntuntum̄ nɔ̄   trousers is looking for
   na ɔɔhwɛhwɛ́ wɔ̨.   you.

5. Ɔbáa bɛ́n na ɔ́ɔsɔ̄ egyą́   Who is that woman carrying
   nɔ̄?   firewood?

   Mīnním ɔbáa nɔ̄, á̀à   I don't know that woman who
   ɔ́ɔsɔ̄ egyą́ nɔ̄.   is carrying the firewood.

6. Ɛhɛ̃́ na kúruwà á̀à mɛ̃   Where is the cup that my mother
   mãamɛ̃́ dɛ̨ mãa mɛ̃ nɔ̄   gave me?
   wɔ?

   Kúruwà á̀à wɔ̨́ mãamɛ̃́   The cup that your mother give
   dɛ̨ mãa wɔ̨ nɔ̄ abɔ́.   you got broken.

7. Hwắñ na ɔfáà ŋhốmã áà   Who took the book that was
     ɛdá ɔpốn nố sɔ́?   lying on the table?
     Ɔsɔ́fɔ́ɔ nố fáà ŋhốmã   The preacher took the book
     áà   ɛdá ɔpốn nố   that was lying on the
     sɔ́?   table.

8. Abarɛmáà bɛ̃n na wɔ́ nế   Who was that boy you were
     nố kasa?   talking to?
     Abarɛmáà nố yɛ mí   That boy is one of my students.
     sukúùfúo nố mú baakố.

9. Ąkoñ̃ñúą́ áà n(a) esí   Where is the chair that was
     mfɛ́nsɛ̀rɛ̨́áṅ̀ nố wɔ   under the window?
     hế?
     Yɛtɔņŋ ąkoñ̃ñúą́ nố   That chair was sold to a
     mãa ɔbáa áà ɔbaa   woman who came yesterday.
     ɛhá nnɛ́ra.

10. Mfɛ̃nsɛrɛ nố kyɛ̨rɛ́   Which direction does the
     ɛhế?   window face?
     Mfɛ̃nsɛrɛ nố kyɛ̨rɛ́   The window faces the street.
     abɔntɛ̃́ñ.

New words

     tíìm   team
     ɔsɔ́fɔ́ɔ (pl. a-)   preacher, minister, priest

Question and Answer Drill B

1. Wǫ́wò tuntuḿ anǎa
   fítaa?

   Mɛ̃wɔ kokɔɔ́ ŋkɔ̃aa.

   Do you have either a black one
   or a white one?

   I have only red ones.

2. Hwǎ́n na ɔ́ɔkɔ kúro
   kɛsǫ́ɛ mǔ?

   Yɛŋ mǔ baakɔ̃ ɛɛkɔ́
   kúro kɛsǫ́ɛ mǔ.

   Who is going into the city?

   Either he or I am going into
   the city.

3. Hwǎ́n na ɔkǎ́ày sɛ́ɛ́
   ɔ́mmára?

   Kofí nɛ̃ Ámmá mǔ
   baakɔ̃ na ɛŋkǎ́ày
   sɛ́ɛ́ ɔ́mmára.

   Who asked him to come?

   Neither Kofi nor Amma asked
   him to come.

4. Ɛdǫ́ɛ̃n ntí na wǫ́kɔɔ́ hɔ́?

   Mɛ̃kɔɔ hɔ́ kɔhánɛ̃
   dǎ́ñ.

   Why did you go there?

   I went there to rent a room?

5. Wúhǔu barǫ́má áà na
   wǫ́phwǫ́hwɛ nɔ̃?

   Má̧ŋhǔ barǫ́má áà na
   mɛ̃ehwǫ́hwɛ nɔ̃.

   Did you find the man you were
   looking for?

   I couldn't find the man I
   was looking for.

6. Wǫ́gyǫ́ǫ nnǫ́ɛma áà ɔdǫ́
   baayɛ nɔ̃.

   Mɛ̃gyǫ́ǫ nnǫ́ɛma áà
   ɔdǫ́ baayɛ nɔ̃ bí.

   Did you accept the things he
   brought?

   I accepted some of the things
   he brought.

186

7. Wǫ́ dǎñ nǒ wɔ sǫ́rǫ   Is your room upstairs or
   anɛ́a fǎm̀?   downstairs?

   Mɛ́ dǎñ nǒ wɔ ɛsǫ́rǫ̀   My room is upstairs at the
   hǒ etírı hɔ́.   end /of the hall/.

8. Wǫ́dɛ̀ egyǎ nǒ áà   What are you going to do with
   wǫ́twa̰àyɛ nǒ kɔyɛ́ dɛɛ́ñ?   the wood they cut up?

   Mɛ̃dɛ egyǎ nǒ áà   I'm going to save the firewood
   wǫ́twa̰àyɛ nǒ.   that they cut up.

   rɛ̰kosíe.

9. Wókyɛ̰rɛɛ̀ nǒ sɛ́nɛ̰a   Did you explain to him how to
   yɛhyɛ́ káà asɛ̰.   start the car?

   Da̰abí, Kwa̰kù na   No, but Kwaku explained to
   ɛkyɛ́rɛɛ̀ nǒ sɛ́nɛ̰a   him how to start the car.
   yɛhyɛ́ káà asɛ̰.

10. Wa̰hyıa̰ ŋkɔrɔfóɔ áà ɔtɛ   Have you met the people who
    ɔdǎñ baakɔ́ nǒ m(ú)?   live next door?

    Áà̰ñ, ma̰hyıa̰ ŋkɔrɔfóɔ   Yes, I have met the neighbors.
    áà ɔtɛ ɔdǎñ baakɔ́
    nǒ m(ú).

New words

    há̰nɛ̃̀, há̰ɛ̰̀   to rent, hire

    sıé   to save, keep

    kyɛrɛ́...asɛ̰   to explain, show

    ŋkɔrɔfóɔ   neighbors

Lexical Drill B

1. Éèbíą̀ nsúo bétǫ ansá | It will probably rain before
   na yasáñ ábà. | we get back.

2. Éèbíą̀ nsúo bétǫ **mą̀kyí**. | It will probably rain while
   | I'm out.

3. **Wɔkɔ́o mą̀kyí.** | They fought during my absence.

4. Wɔkɔ́o **wɔ bɛ́pɔ nɔ́ sɔ́.** | They fought a battle on the
   | hilltop.

5. **Osɪɪ dáñ** wɔ bɛ́pɔ nɔ́ | He built a house on top of the
   sɔ́. | hill.

6. Osɪɪ dáñ **wɔ bɛ́pɔ nɔ́** | He built a house at the foot of
   asę̀. | the mountain.

7. **Ą̀subúrá da** bɛ́pɔ nɔ́ | There's a well at the bottom of
   asę̀. | the mountain.

8. Ą̀subúrá da **ɔdáñ nɔ́** | There's a well on the other
   ñkyɛ́ñ. | side of the house.

9. **Obí** rę̀twę́ñ wɔ wɔ ɔdáñ | There's someone waiting for
   nɔ́ ñkyɛ́ñ. | you on the other side of the
   | house.

10. **Ebínɔ̃m** rę̀twę́ñ wɔ wɔ | Some of the people are waiting
    ɔdáñ nɔ́ ñkyɛ́ñ. | for you on the other side of
    | the house.

11. **Nkɔ̀rɔfóɔ bí** rę̀twę́ñ wɔ | There are some people waiting
    wɔ ɔdáñ nɔ́ ñkyɛ́ñ. | for you on the other side
    | of the house.

Lexical Drill C

1. Ɔmãa mẽ nantɛ́ yíye̊.   He bade me farewell.

2. Ɔmãa mẽ ṇhɔ́mã bí áà   He gave me a book about Ghana.
   ɛfá Ghánà hɔ́.

3. Mẽ nsá ákã̀ ṇhɔ́mã bí   I have received a book about
   áà ɛfá Ghánà hɔ́.   Ghana.

4. Mẽ nsá ákã̀ sɪká áà   I have received the money
   ohɛ́nɛ nɔ́ dɛ mãnéè̊   which the chief sent me.
   mẽ nɔ́.

5. Obí ą́wĩ̀ą sɪká áà   Someone has stolen the money
   ohɛ́nɛ nɔ́ dɛ mãnéè̊   which the chief sent me.
   mẽ nɔ́.

6. Obí ą́wĩ̀ą sɪká áà mẽ́   Someone has stolen all the
   nsá ká̊àyɛ nɔ́.   money that I received.
   ñyĩnã́a.

7. Masɛ́ɛ sɪká áà mẽ́ nsá   I have used up all the money
   ká̊àyɛ nɔ́ ñyĩnã́a.   that I received.

8. Masɛ́ɛ mẽ pénsɛrɛ áà   I have used up my last pencil.
   ákà nɔ́.

9. Wɐfá mẽ pénsɛrɛ ʌ̂à   He has taken my last pencil.
   ákà nɔ́.

10. Wɐfá saá kwã́ñ yí sɔ́   He has used this road before.
    da.

189

New words

    kã   to touch, come in contact with, come to, reach

    mãnế, mãnã   to send, receive

    w̌ıạ́   to steal

    sẹ   to spend, use up; damage, ruin

Lexical Drill D

1. Métuạ wọ pón baakố   I will pay you one pount to
   mã wapẹrá dắn mũ   clean this room.
   há.

2. Pón baakố suạ mã mẽ   One pound is not enough for me
   sɛ́ɛ̀ mẽpẹrá dắn mũ   to clean this room.
   há.

3. Pón baakố suạ mã   One pound isn't enough for a
   ataadẹ́ɛ fọ́fọ́rọ.   new suit.

4. Saá ntamã́ yí yế mã   This material is suitable for
   ataadẹ́ɛ fọ́fọ́rọ.   a new dress.

5. Saá ntamã́ yí nế mẽ   This material goes well with
   kyế yı na ɛɛkó.   my hat.

6. Mẽ táẹ̀ yí nế matáádẹɛ   This tie of mine goes well with
   fọ́fọ́rọ nố na ɛɛkó.   my new suit.

7. Mẽ táẹ̀ yí nế matáádẹɛ   This tie of mine and my new
   fọ́fọ́rọ nố fırı   suit are from Europe.
   Ạburokyírı.

8. <u>Mawɔ́fɔonõm fırı</u>   My parents are from Europe.
   Ạburokyírı.

9. Mawɔ́fɔonõm fırı   My parents are back from
   Ạburokyírı <u>ábà</u>.   Europe.

10. <u>Ɔdę ņkęrá fırı</u>   He brought a message from
    <u>Ạburokyírı ábà</u>.   Europe.

New word

   suą   to be little, few, ınsufficıent

Unit 20

Basic Dialogue

-A-

kyiá	to greet, shake hands, welcome; bet, wager
1 Owúrà Ménsâh, mɛ̃dɛ̨ mɪ́ ñúɑ̨ yí rɪbekyɪɑ́ wɔ́.	Mr. Mensah, I want to present my brother to you.

-B-

| 2 Yɛfɛɾɛ́ wɔ sɛ̃ʔ | What's your name? |

-C-

| 3 Yɛfɛɾɛ́ mɛ̃ Kwɑ̨kú Bónsù. | My name is Kwaku Bonsu. |

-B-

| 4 Wɔ́tɛ̨̀ kúrom há anɑ̃́ɑ̀ʔ Ɛsɪɑ̃́nɛ̀ sɛ́ɛ̀ mɛ̃ñhyɪɑ̨̀ wɔ da. | Do you live in the city? I've never met you before. |

-C-

| 5 Dɑ̨ɑ̨bí, mɛ̃ntɛ̨́ há. Mɛ̃tɛ̨ Kumásɛ̨. Mɛ̃bɛsɛɾáà mɪ́ ñúɑ̨. | No, I don't live here. I live at Kumasi. I'm /here/ visiting my brother. |

-B-

| 6 Wúnɪ̃m owúrà Kwaɓɛ̨ná Ántwɪ̀ʔ Ɔtɔ́ kookóò wɔ Kumásɛ̨. | Do you know Kwabena Antwi? He is a cocoa buyer at Kumasi. |

-C-

| 7 Ɑ̃́ɑ̨̀ñ, mɪ̃nɪ̃m nɔ̃́. Ɔtɔ́ kookóò fɪrɪ mɛ̃́ papá ñkyɛ̃́ñ. | Yes, I know him. He buys cocoa from my father. |

192

-B-

8   Dá bɛ́n na wóbɛsãñ ákɔ̀   When do you return to Kumasɪ?
    Kumásɛ̨?

-C-

9   Ɔkyɛ́na anɔpã́.   Tomorrow morning.

-B-

10 Nantɛ̨́ yíyɛ̇̀.   Goodbye. Have a good trɪp.
                                    Farewell.

-C-

11 Yɛ̨ɛ̨ owúrà.   Yes sɪr.

Notes

1. /Nantɛ̨́ yíyɛ̨̀/, 'Farewell', ɪs used when someone ɪs goɪng on
a trɪp. /Makɛ̨́ra wɔ/, 'Goodbye', 'I'm takɪng leave of you' ɪs
used when you expect to see the person agaɪn faɪrly soon.

Pattern Drɪll A

1. Mɛ̃paw kyɛ́w, mã́ mɛ̃   Please let me ɪntroduce you
    mfáẁ ñkyɛ̨́rɛ̀ ɔpañyín yí.   to thɪs man.

2. Mɛ̇paw kyɛ́w, __mã́__   Please let me show you where
    __mɛ̃́ñkyɛ̨rɛ̀ẁ nɛ̨a ɛwɔ.__   ɪt ɪs.

3. Mɛ̇paw kyɛ́w, __fa nkwã́n__   Please pass me the soup.
    __mã́ mɛ̃ nɔ́.__

4. Mɛ̃paw kyɛ́w, __mã́ mɛ̃̇__   Please let me have some of
    __fufúo nɔ́ bí.__   the fufu.

5. Mɛ̇paw kyɛ́w, __kyɛ̨rɛ́ mɛ̃__   Please show me where ɪt ɪs.
    __nɛ̨a ɛwɔ.__

6. Mɛ̃paw kyɛ́w, kã́ kyɛrɛ
   nõ sɛ́ɛ̀ ɔ́ɔŋkɔ.

Please tell him to leave.

7. Mɛ̃paw kyɛ́w, kã́ kyɛré
   nõ sɛ́ɛ̀ mɛ̃wɔ há.

Please tell him I am here.

8. Mɛ̃paw kyɛ́w, kotó
   núusɔpèpa mã́ mɛ̃.

Please go buy me a newspaper.

9. Mɛ̃paw kyɛ́w, twɛ̨n mɛ̃
   wɔ há.

Please wait for me here.

10. Mɛ̃paw kyɛ́w, bɛfá mɛ̃
    nnónwòtwɛ̨.

Please come for me at eight
o'clock.

New words

     ɔpañyíñ (pl. m-fɔ́ɔ̀)   adult, grown person

     núusɔpèpa   newspaper

Lexical Drill A

1. Yɛtɔɔ akwadaá nṍ
   díñ Asamõá.

We named the baby Asamoa.

2. Yɛtɔɔ pṍn nṍ mũ ansã́
   na yɛkɔɔ yɛ.

We locked the door before we
left.

3. Wansã́n ammá ansã́ na
   yɛkɔɔyɛ.

He didn't come back before
we left.

4. Wansã́n ammá kopɛ̀m
   nnón mmiensã́ né fã́.

He didn't come back until
three thirty.

5. Mą̃ññyą̃́ kwã́ñ mañyé
   kɔpɛ̨́m nnón mmiensã́
   né fã́.

I didn't get a chance to do
it until three thirty.

6. Mąññyá kwáñ maŋkogyé   I didn't get a chance to go
   vísà mẽdę bέkɔ   get a visa for Ghana.
   Ghánà nɔ́.

7. Ɛsɛ sɛ́ɛ́ mẽkogyé vísà   I have to go get a visa for
   mẽdę bέkɔ Ghánà nɔ́.   Ghana.

8. Ɛsɛ sɛ́ɛ́ mẽkogyé   I've got to go get my suit
   matáádęɛ áà ɛwɔ   which is at the tailor's.
   téèla hɔ́ nɔ́.

9. Wúbenyá̧ kwáñ akogyé   Will you have time to go
   matáádęɛ áà ɛwɔ   get my suit which is at
   téèla hɔ́ nɔ́?   the tailor's?

10. Wúbenyá̧ kwáñ abǫá   Will you have time to help
    mẽ má mahyęhyέ mẽ   me pack?
    nnę́ɛmá̧ʋ

New words

   kopę́m   until, as far as
   vísà   visa
   téèla   tailor

Question and Answer Drill A

1. Sέn na wǫ́gyę dí sɛ́ɛ́   How much do you think she
   ɔbégyę́?   will charge?
   . Mẽgyę́ dí sɛ́ɛ́ pɔ́n   I think that she will be
     nnáñ bésǫ́ nąní.   pleased with four pounds.
                                ('I take use that four
                                pounds will catch her eye.')

2. Mmɔfára yí déɛ, wɔ́dɛ̀   What about the children, are
   woŋ béko?   they going?

   Mmɔfára yí déɛ, woŋ   As for the children, they
   né woŋ mãamé na   will go with their
   ɛbékɔ.   mother.

3. Mɛ́rɛ °dɔ́dɔ sɛ́n na wúnĩm   How long have you know him?
   nő?

   Mĩnĩm nő fɪrɪ mẽ   I have known him since I
   mmɔfáraasɛ̣.   was a child.

4. Poŋkó bɛ́n na wɔ́betɔ̣   Which horse are you going to
   ñkyɪ̣ɑ́ wo nő sɔ̣́?   bet on?

   Mɛ́tɔ̣ ñhyɪ̣ɑ́ wo poŋkó   I'm going to bet on the
   áà ogyɪna   horse in the middle.
   mfínɪmfɪnɪ́ nő.

5. Sɪká sɛ́n na wúñyaá   How much money did you win at
   yɛ wɔ résɛ̣s(ɛ̣)?   the races?

   Mĩñyɑ̣́ɑ̣ pɔ́ŋ mpɛ̣́m   I won a thousand pounds
   nné.   today.

6. Sɪká sɛ́n na wɔ́sɛɛ̀ wo   How much did you lose at the
   résɛ̣s(ɛ̣)?   races?

   Mɛ̃sɛ́ɛ̀ mĩ́ sɪká mɛ̃wo   I lost all the money I had.
   ñyĩńáa.

7. Dá bɛ́ŋ na woń nő   When did they get married?
   warɛ̣́ɛ̣̀yɛ.

   Woń nő warɛ̣́ɛ̣̀ anɔpá   They got married this
   yí áà.   morning.

196

8. Wón nố ñyá̰á̰ akyédȩ́ bí?   Did they receive any gifts?

    Wón nố ñyá̰á̰ akyέdȩ́   They received many gifts.

    pìì.

9. Ɛdȩ́έn na wó̧dȩ̀ hyɛɛ woŋ?   What did you give them?

    Mẽkyɛɛ woŋ mpȩ́rétȩ̀.   I gave them dishes.

10. Ɛdȩ́έn na wó̧pè sέέ mẽdȩ́   What do you want me to give

    kyέw?   you?

    Mẽpɛ sέέ wó̧kyɛ mẽ   I want you to give me your

    wó̧ fótó̧.   picture.

New words

    sɔ   to drip; kindle; try; seal

    sɔ ą̰ní   to please, satisfy

    dó̧dɔ   how many, how much

    mfínìmfìní   in the middle of

    résȩ́s(ȩ́)   races

    warȩ́   to marry, get married

    akyédȩ́ (ákyέdȩ́) (pl. ñ-)   gift

    pȩ́rètȩ́ (pl. m-)   plate, dish

    fótó̧ (pl. m-)   photograph

Lexical Drill B

1. Ɔkó ą̰fúom ákòduá̰   He's gone to the farm to

    ą̰burɔ́.   plant corn.

2. Ɔkohwȩ́hwɛ bą̰ą̰bí átȩ̀ná̰.   He's gone to look for a place

                                   to live.

3. Mẽepɛ bą̰ą̰bí átȩ̀ná̰.   I'm looking for a place to live.

197

4. Méɛpɛ obí mã ɔdɛ mẽ
   ákɔ̀ ewĭmúhyɛ̃n
   gyınábɛ̀a.

I'm looking for someone to
take me to the airport.

5. Ehíá̱ obí mã ɔdɛ mẽ
   ákɔ̀ ewĭmúhyɛ̃n
   gyınábɛ̀a.

I need someone to
take me to the airport.

6. Ehíá̱ sıká áà mẽdɛ
   bɛ́tɔ ạduạnɛ̱́.

I need some money to buy
food.

7. Obısáà sıká áà ɔdɛ̱́
   bɛ́tɔ̀ ạduạnɛ̱́.

She asked for money to buy
food.

8. Obısáà mẽ sɛ́ɛ̀ métúmı
   ábɛsɛraà nɔ̃́.

She asked me if I can visit
her.

9. Wúnîm sɛ́ɛ̀ métúmı
   akosɛ̱́ra nɔ̃́?

Do you know if I can visit
her?

10. Wúnîm sɛ́nɛ̀a yɛbɛ́yɛ
    nay(ɛ) ạ́hũ nɔ̃́?

Do you know how she can be
found?

New word

　ạburó　(abúrò)

corn, maize

Pattern Drill B

1. Ogyına káà esı duạ̱́
   nɔ̃́ hɔ̃́.

He is standing by the car
next to the tree.

2. Nsúo nɔ̃́ sı káà esı duạ̱́
   nɔ̃́ hɔ̃́.

The bucket of water is by the
car near the tree.

3. Nsúo nɔ̃́ sı ɔpɔ̃nɔ̃́ nɔ̃́ sɔ̱́
   wo mfɛ́nsɛrɛ nɔ̃́ asɛ̱.

The bucket of water is sitting
on the table under the window.

198

4. Nhõmã áà yaboa anõ gú
   opõnõ nõ só wo
   mfénsęrę nõ asę.

A stack of papers is lying on
the table under the window.

5. Nhõmã áà yaboa anõ gú
   adáká mú sı ąkõññúá
   nõ só.

There's a stack of papers in
the box on the chair.

6. Safõwá nõ da adáká mú
   sı ąkõññúá nõ só.

The key is lying in the box
on the chair.

7. Safõwá nõ da opõnąnım̀
   wɔ fám̀ hó.

The key is lying on the floor
in front of the door.

8. Mĩgyaą nõ opõnąnım̀ wɔ
   fám̀ hó.

I left it on the floor in
front of the door.

9. Mĩgyaą nõ opõnõ nõ só
   wɔ nhõmã só.

I left it on the table on top
of a book.

10. Mĩgyı́ dı́ séé ɛda opõnõ
    nõ só wɔ nhõmã só.

I think it is on the table on
top of a book.

New words

        opõnąnım̀   front of a door,(door's face)

Pattern Drill C

   1. Mẽdę káà hõ nnęɛmã   I sent him the automobile
      mãnéè nnéra.   parts yesterday.

   2. Mẽdę káà hõ nnęɛmã   I repaired my car with the
      fofóro nõ sıésıeè   new parts.
      mẽ káà nõ.

199

3. Mɛ̃dɛ̨ <u>nɛ̃ pɛ́n nɔ̃</u>
   <u>kyɛ̨rɛ́wẁ mĩ díñ.</u>
       I wrote my name with his pen.

4. Mɛ̃dɛ̨ <u>nɔ̃ kohũú dɔ́kɛ̨ta</u>
   <u>nɔ̃̂.</u>
       I took him to see the doctor.

5. Mɛ̃dɛ̨ <u>nɔ̃ koɔ mɛ̃a</u>
   <u>okosíesieè mɛ̨ káà</u>
   <u>nɔ̃̂.</u>
       I sent him to fix my car.

6. Mɛ̃dɛ̨ <u>sékáñ síñsíñà</u>
   <u>mɛ̨ pɛ́nsɛ̨rɛ̨ anɔ̨́.</u>
       I sharpened my pencil with
        a knife.

7. Mɛ̃dɛ̨ <u>pɛ́nsɛ̨rɛ̨ tɔ̨ɔ adáká</u>
   <u>nɔ̃ sɔ̨́.</u>
       I put the pencil on the box.

8. Mɛ̃dɛ̨ <u>nɔ̃ bą́ą ądwúma.</u>
       I brought him to work with
        me.

9. Mɛ̃dɛ̨ <u>natáádɛ̨ɛ komɛ̃̀a</u>
   <u>wahyɛ̨mán.</u>
       I sent his clothes to the
        laundryman.

10. Mɛ̃dɛ̨ <u>násɛ̀m nɔ̃ ákɔ̀tɔ̨</u>
   <u>ɔpañyín nɔ̃ ąním.</u>
       I have presented his case to
        the boss.

New words

    síñsíñ
                   to cut, carve, sharpen, peel

    wahyɛ̨mán
                   washerman, launderer

2. /dɛ̨́ɛ/, 'as for', 'concerning', 'what about' is used after
a noun to give strong emphasis or special prominence to it.
See Question and Answer Drill A, sentence 2.

3. /dɔ̨́dɔ̨/ is usually // dodow//.

4. When two locations are specified for an object, usually /áà.
precedes the second location; but as shown in Pattern Drill B,
it is possible to omit the /áà/. For example, in sentence 1 /áà/
may occur between /káà/ and /esɪ/. Compare Unit 15, note 7.

5. /sɪ/, means 'to be in a vertical position'. If water is to
/sɪ/, it must be in a container. See Pattern Drill B, sentence 2.
The same would be true of an item like a box of salt.

GLOSSARY - This vocabulary is alphabetized according to the stem consonant and not according to the prefixes, e.g., /ɛdá/, 'day', is alphabetized under 'd'.

áà	which, that, what, where
(sɛ)... áà	if, when, whenever
ba	to come, arrive
bɛrá	Come (imperative)
dɛ... ba	bring
ɔbá (pl. m-)	child, young one
baá	to open
ɔbáa (pl. m-)	woman, female
ɔbábarɛmá	son, male child
bąąbí (pl. -nŏm)	a place, somewhere
baakó	one
baakó nó	the second one, the other one
báęgę	bag, sach, briefcase
abáñ (báñ) (pl. m-)	a large or strong building, the government
yɛ́ abáñ ądwùma	to work for the government, be a civil servant
bañkyé	cassava
ɔbarɛmá (pl. m-)	man, male
ąbáti (pl. m-)	shoulder
abaawá (pl. m-)	servant girl, maid
abáawa (pl. m-)	girl
bayɛ́rɛ	yam
bɛ-	to come for, to come to do
bɛ́-	will, shall, future time
bɛ́yɛ (with numerals)	approximately
(with prices)	the total is
bęá (bęa) (pl. m-)	place; manner
bɛ́ñ	what, which, what kind of
bɛņ	to be near, approaching
Bęnada	Tuesday

202

bɛ̃ŋkũm (bɛ̃ŋkum)	left, left side
bɛ́pɔ	mountain, hilltop
bɛrɛ́	to bring something to a person
bɛrɛ̂	to fatigue, grow weary or tired
bɛ́rɛ (pl. m-)	time
mmɛ́r(e) áà	when, time that
bɛrɛɛoo, bɛrɛɛw	soft, slow, mild
bɛtɛɛ	soft, tender
bí	a, an, some, any
obí	someone, anyone
éebíà	perhaps, maybe
bíara	every, each
obiara	everyone
ebío	again
bɪrɪbí	something, anything; nothing (in negative sentence)
bíruù	blue
bɪsá	to ask, question
bɔ	to hit, strike, set in motion come in contact with; break, destroy, shoot; tie, tie up tie on
bɔ... páanɛɛ	to give a shot of medicine
ɛbɔ́ɔ	price; store, pit, seed
bɔa	to group or be grouped together in a bunch or group
bɔábɔ̀a	to be distributed in groups
bɔa	to help, aid, assist
bɔá	to lie, tell a lie
bɔaá	bundle, package
ɔbɔáfɔ́ɔ (pl. a-)	helper, assistant
abɔfára (pl. m-)	child
bɔ́kɛtɛ	bucket
bokɔɔ	soft, tender, cheap
bɔ́ɔl	ball

ạbomúu	stew
abọŋkó (bọŋkó) (pl. m-)	shrimps
abọntéñ (pl. m-)	street; outdoors, outside
bọrọdéɛ	plantain, European yam
bọrọdọ	bread
Bọrọfọ́	English, European language
Bọrọfọká	English language, spoken English
bɔ́ɔ́sọ	bus
bɔ́ɔ́sọgyınábẹ̣a	bus station, bus stop
bɔ́ɔ́sọtapọ	bus stop
bu	to bend, curve; break, break off; decide, judge
bué	to spread, open, flatten out
búùku, búùkuú	book
ạburó (abúrò)	corn, maize
Ạburokyírı	Europe, America
Oburoní (pl. Abọrɔfọ́)	a European
da	to sleep, lie, rest, be in a prone position
da asẹ	to lie down; thank
dẹda	to lie about
ɛdá (pl. n-)	day
dáa	always
dạạbí, dạbí	no, not, never
adáká	box, case, trunk, suitcase
adamfọ (adámfọ́) (pl. n-nõm)	friend
ɛdáñ (dáñ) (pl. n-na-)	building, house, room
dẹ́, dẹ́ɛ	to have, possess; be, be in a state of; keep on, continue; cause, make; take, require
dẹ́ɛ	concerning, as to, with reference to
dɛ	sweet
adẹ́ɛ (dẹ́ɛ) (pl. nnẹ́ɛma)	thing

ɔdéɛ̀	yam
dea	he who, he whose, that which, where
dedaw	already
dédàw	old, encient
ɛdɛ́n	what, how
ɛdɛ̀čñ = ɛdɛ̀ɛ̀ béñ	
adesúá	learning, study, education
dɪ	to eat, employ, use, spend
dɪdí	to eat
dɪ asę	to agree on a price, strike a bargain
adɪ	out, outside, outdoors
adɪdę́ɛ	use, enjoyment, benefit
adɪdɪadídì	the enjoyment of eating
adɪdí	eating, to eat
adíhọ, adɪwo	the yard around a house; outside, outdoors
déñ	hard, difficult, expensive
edíñ	name; reputation, fame
dọdọ	how many, how much
dókęta	doctor, physician
ɔdóñ (nòñ) (pl. n-)	bell
donhwéręfã	half-hour
donhwéręw (pl. n-)	hour
aduanę́ (pl. n-)	food
du, duru	to descend, arrive
edú	ten
duá (nnuá)	tree, stick, wood
aduokọróñ	ninety
aduanáñ	forty
aduonū	twenty
aduonúm	fifty
aduasá	thirty
aduosíá	sixty

ạduosɔ́ŋ	seventy
ạduowɔ́twẹ	eighty
duru	heavy
ạdúru	medicine, herbs
dwạ	to cut up, cut in pieces
dwẹrẹ	to tie up, bind
dwɛrẹ	to crush, mash
dwọ	to cool, be cool
Dwọɔda	Monday
edwómũ (pl. (e)ññwómũ)	market, market place
ạdwúma (ạdwùma) (pl. ññwúma)	work, job
ạdwúmayɛ	work, working, to work
ɛɛ	a question marker
ɛ́ɛ̀	yes
fa	to take, take away, seize, obtain, get; up to, as far as; by means of; about, concerning
fã	to be hoarse
ɛfá	earth, soil, dirt
ofá (fá) (pl. ạfũạfá)	half, piece, other side, other part
efám̀	ground, floor, bottom; below
Faransẹ́ɛ	French
ofásù (pl. ạ-)	wall
fɛ	pretty, nice, beautiful
afẹ́ (pl. mfíe)	year
ạ́fèɪ	now
ạ́fèɪ ansá na... bɛ́-	to be about to
mfɛ́nsẹrẹ	window
fẹ́rà	to mix
fẹrɛ́	to call, name; telephone

fı, fırı	to be from, from, to leave, leave from
fı... asę	to begin, start
ofíe	house, home
Fíèda	Friday
mfínìmfìní	in the middle of
fıtá	to fan a fire
fítaa	white, clear
fìtáę̀	bellows, woven fan
fǫ	cheap, plenty, plentiful
fǫ́fǫ́rǫ	new, another
mfoní	picture
fǫ́tbɔ̀ɔl	soccer
fótò (pl. m-)	photograph
fuą	to hold, seize
fuą́	single, one
fufúo	fufu, a Bhanaian food
fúfuo	white
ꜰfúǫ, (fúo) (pl. m-)	farm, field
fura	to wear or put Ghanian dress
agǫǫ	Is anybody there?
	Quiet please. (said to a group)
	Let me pass.
ŋgǫ́	palm oil, cooking oil
gorǫ, goru	to play
agorǫ́bęa	place to play, playground
gu	to pour; scatter, be located in groups, be scattered
gugu	to be scattered about
oguáñ (pl. ñ-)	sheep
guą̀ąsǫ	market, market place
guą́ąsǫkwáñ	market road, the road to the market

207

ɛyą	to leave, quit, forsake; send away, accompany
ągyá (ągyá) (pl. -nŏm)	father
egyą́ (gyą́)	firewood
ogyą́	fire
ɛyę	to take, receive, accept; take internally; charge a price
gyę di	to believe
gyına	to stop, stand, rest, come to a standing on, upright position
gyınągyına	to stand about
gyínabẹ́a	stopping place, station, harbor
ahá	weariness; an afternoon greeting
ɛhá (pl. ɛ-nŏm)	here; this
ɔha	hundred
ahabámmọ́nọ	green
ahabáń (pl.ŋ-)	leaf, foilage
háę̀	to rent, hire
ahé	how much, how many, how long
ɛhé (pl. ɛ-nŏm)	where
ɛhéfá	where
hɛ́lọ̀	hello
ahę́mfıe	palace, king's house, chief's house
ɛhéna (pl. -nŏm)	who, whom, whose
ɔhę́nę (hę́nę) (pl. a-nŏm)	king, chief
ɔhę́nęfıe	king's house than palace
híą́	to distress, trouble, need, require
ɛhɔ́ (pl. ɛ-nŏm)	there; that; from
ɛhɔ́	the whole body; exterior; at, by, near
ahŏɔdéń	strength
ɔhɔ́họ̀ọ̀ (pl. a-)	stranger, foreigner, guest
ŋhómá (hómá) (pl. ŋgómá)	skin, hide; leather, book, letter
ŋhómákyęréw	letter writing, to write letters

hóró, hohóró	to wash, launder
hũ, hũnṹ	to see
ahúhuró́	hot
hwɛ	to look at; look after; consider; know
hwę	to fall, tumble, beat
hwę asę	to fall down
hwęę	something, anything
hwɛ́fɔɔ (pl. a-)	caretaker, supervisor
hwęhwɛ́	to search for, look for; want, desire
hwęrę́	to consume, use up, pass time
hwié	to pour out of
hyáin	to shine, polish
hyɛ	to insert, put in; put on, wear
hyɛ... mã́	to fill up
hyę	to burn, be on fire; be hot (weathe)
hyęhyę́	to arrange, adjust; fit out, equip
hyɛ̃ñ	to blow a musical instrument
ɛhyɛ̃ñ (pl. a-)	boat, ship
hyɛnņ	bright, brilliant
hyęrɛ̃ñ	to penetrate, get through, shine
hyiá̧	to meet, assemble; agree, be in accord
ñhyiá̧m	meeting, conference, assembly
ñhyiamṹ dã́ñ	assembly hall, conference room
hyúù	shoe, pair of shoes
ka	to remain, be left
ká̧	to speak, say, talk
kã kyęrɛ́	to tell, give information to
ká̧... hó̃ asɛ́m	to talk about, discuss

209

kã	to touch, come in contact with, come to, reach, receive
ɛká (pl. ŋ-)	debt, something which is lacking
kaá	ring, bracelet
káà	car, automobile
káàká	automobile driving, to drive a car
káñ	to count, read
kéñkáñ	to read, count
kanẹa	light, light fixture
kápẹrɛ	penny
kasa	to talk
áŋkasa	self
ŋkátéɛ	peanut, groundant
akéñkáñ	reading, to read
kẹrà	to leave, take leave of, say goodbye
kẹrá	soul
ŋkẹrá (ŋkẹrà)	message
ŋkẹrábẹa	fate, destiny, manner of death
ɔkẹrámáñ (pl. a-)	dog
kẹraàtaá (pl. n-)	paper, sheet of paper, letter
kesẹɛ (pl. a-)	by, large; great, grand
ɔkẹtẹkẹ (pl. ŋ-)	hyena; locomotive, train
kẹtẹwa (pl. ŋ-)	small, little
kẹtwaa	very small
kɔ	to go, go away, go to do
dẹ... kɔ	to send away, cause to go
kɔ sɔ́	to keep on, continue
kɔ́	one
kɔ́	to fight
ŋkɔ́aa	only, just
akɔ́kɔ́ (pl. ŋ-)	chicken
kɔkɔɔ́	red, orange, reddish brown, purple
kookóò (kóòkoò)	cocoa

ɔkóm	hunger
akókoserádɛ́ɛ́	yellow, light tan
akõññúá (pl. ŋ-)	chair, stool
akontá	brother-in-law
akóntáá	arithmetic, reckoning, accounting
kopém	until, as far as
korá	to save, hide, conceal, keep
kórà	co-wife
koraá	colabash
korɔ	one
nkorofɔ́ɔ	neighbors
ɛnkorṍn	nine
kosí	until, up to
kóòtu	coat
kótà	quart
kotɔkɔ	brave companions; able teammates
kotokú (pl. ŋ-)	pocket, bag
kúm	to kill, execute; cause to
okúnu (kúnu) (pl. -ñÕm)	husband, sister's husband
akurá (pl. n-)	mouse
akuraá	village, country town
okuraáséni (pl. ŋ-fɔ́ɔ)	villager
kúro	town, city, village
kuru	to thatch, build a thatch roof
kúru	a sore
ekúruwá	cup, pitcher
akutú	orange
akutúdie	eating of oranges, to eat oranges, orange-eating
akwadaá (pl. ŋ-)	baby, infant
akwadú	banana
nkwã́ñ	soup
ɔkwã́ñ (pl. a-)	road, path; way, method; opportunity

211

ɔkwãnsiɲ (pl. a-)	mile
ɲkwantá	crossroad, junction, a Y
kwạsíeda	Sunday
kyɛ	to last, ending; divide, separate, share
akyɛ́	a becoming clear or visible, a coming-
ɔkyɛ̃ámɛ (pl. a-)	a chief's spokesman, interpreter
akyɛ́dɛ (ákyɛ́dɛ) (pl. ñ-)	
kyɛ̃ñ	to surpass, pass excel; more than, than
ñkyɛ̃ñ	side; from, apart, by, near
ɔkyɛ́na	tomorrow
ñkyɛ́nɛ	salt
ñkyɛ́nɛñkyɛ́nɛ	salty
kyɛrɛ́	to show, exhibit, point out; advise
kyɛrɛ́ asɛ	to translate; show, explain
kyɛrɛ́ kyɛrɛ	to teach, instruct
ɔkyɛrɛkyɛ́rɛ́fóɔ (pl. a-)	teacher
kyɛrɛ́w	to write
akyɛrɛ́w	writing, to write
kyerɛ́wpóɲ	desk, writing table
ɛkyɛ́w	hat, cap
kyiá	to greet, shake hands, welcome; bet, wager
ạkyí, ạkyíri	the back rear; back, behind; late
kyóòku, kyóòkọ	chalk
óèlɛ, óèyɛrɛ	oil
lɛ́tɛ	letter
lórɛ	truck, lorry, bus, car

mã	to give, present; let, cause; for, on behalf of
εmã	full
hyε... mã	to fill up
mãamé (pl. -nǫm)	mother
ɔmãñ (pl. a-)	nation, people
mãnɛ̃	to send
amannɛ̣ɛ́ (mánnɛ̣ɛ)	message, mission
mmará	law, rule
mɛ̃, mĩ, m-	I, me, my
amɛ̃e	Come in. Speak, we are listening
Mémɛ̣nɛ̣da	Saturday
mɛ́nɛ̣tɛ̣́, mɛ́rɛ̣tɛ̣́ (pl. m-)	minute
mmɛ̣rε	cheap
mmienú	two
mmiensá	three
mɔ́, mú, m-	you, your (pl.)
mmofáraasɛ̣	childhood
mmɔ̃m	rather
mmɔ̃m	agreement, contract
mɔ́mã	to dedicate
mɔ́mã	forbid
amɔ́nɔ̃, ɔmɔ́nɔ̃	fresh, green, unripe, new
emú, mú, mũ, -m	in, inside
emú (pl. a-)	whole, entirety
n-, m-, ñ, ŋ	not
áąñ, áąnɛ̃, ɛ́e	yes
na	and, but; emphasis marker
ná	used to, was formerly in the state of
anáa	or, a question marker

213

anadwǫ́	night
ɛnám	meat, flesh
ńsuomnám	fish
ɛnáń	foot, leg
ɛnnáń	four
ananse̩	spider
nnansá	three days
ananse̩se̩mká	traditional story, 'fairy tale'
nanté̩	to walk, go on foot
na̩ntwie (na̩ntwìe) (pl. a-)	a head of cattle
nnawótwe̩	a week
ne̩	to be, to consist of
né	and, with
ɔné = ɔnɔ́ né	
nẽ, nĩ, n-	his, hers, its
nné, ɛnné	today
ne̩a	he who, that which, he whose, where
nnéra, nnóra	yesterday
nni	negative of di and wɔ
a̩ní	eye; color
nifá (nifá)	right, right side
nĩm	to know, understand
a̩nìm	face, countenance, front; before, in front of
onípa (pl. n-)	person, individual
anɔ́	mouth; edge, brim; beginning
ɛnɔ́, ɛ-, e-	it, they, them
ɔnɔ́, nɔ́, ɔ-, o-	he, she, it, they, him, her, them; when
nóá	to boil, to cook by boiling
nóm	to drink
anõmãá (anòmãa) (pl. n-)	bird
anɔpá	morning, in the morning
anɔpáa̩dùané̩	breakfast

214

ntí	therefore, because
ɛdɛɛ́n ntí	why
oñúą́ (ñúą̀))pl. ą̀-nõ̌m)	brother, sister, sibling
oñúąbaa (ñúąbàa) (pl. ñ̃ñ̃úąmmáa)	sister
oñúąbárẹmá (ñúąbarẹma)	brother, male sibling
(pl. ñ̃ñ̃úąmmárẹmá)	
enúm	five
ñyą̃	to get, acquire, receive, obtain
ñ̃ñyą̃ plus another verb	'not yet
sɛ ñyą̃ ...àa	as soon as
ñyą̃ kwą̃́ñ	to have an opportunity
nyą́n	to ware
ñyĩ́ñáa	all
oo	an emphasis marker
pa	to pass by, more along
pa	to take off, skim, scrape off; beg, beseech
mẽpaw kyɛ́w	please
pá, pápa	good, much
pápaapa, pápapapa	very good
mpá	bed, couch, mattress
mpabǫá (mpábǫ̀a)	shoe, pair of shoes
páanẹɛ (pl. m-)	needle
páanǫ	bread
ɔpáñyíñ	adult, old person, person of rank; old, aged
papa	a woven palm, leaf fan
papá (pápa) (pl. -nõ̌m)	father

215

pɛ	to like, be fond of, want, seek, provide, try to get
pɛ́	exactly, only, precisely, thorouglhy
pɛɛ	near, close to
apɛ̣m (pl. m-)	thousand
pɛ́n (pɛ̀n)	pen
pɛ́n̦ (pl. m-)	once, one time, ever, before, time, occassion
pɛ́nsɛ̣re	pencil
pɛpà	paper
pɛrá	to sweep
pɛráɛ̣	brown
pɛ́rɛ̀tɛ̣ (pl. m-)	plate, dish
ampesie	Ampesi, a Ghanaian food
pɛtɛ́roò dɔ́mpɔ̣	filling station, petrol dump
pii	much, many
pirá	to injure, be injured
ɛpɔ́ (pl. m-)	joint, bump, knob
ɛpɔ̣́	ocean, sea
mpɔ̣anɔ̣́, ɛpɔ̣anɔ̣́	seaside, seashore
pɔ́n̦	pound sterling
pɔ́n̦	to go away, cease, stop; disjoin, separate
ɔpɔ̃́n̦ (pl. a-)	door, gate; table, desk
ɔpɔnkɔ́ (pɔ́nkɔ) (pl. mpɔnkɔ́)	horse
ɔpɔ̃́nõ (pɔ̃́nõ) (pl. m-)	table, desk
pɔ́rosì	police
pɔ́rosìnì (pl. m- fɔ̣́ɔ or a̧-fɔ̣́ɔ)	policeman
pɔ́suɔfɛ̣sɛ̣	post office
rɛ̣-, ri-	progressive action, with act of
rɛ́sɛ̣s(ɛ̣)	races
rɔ́ódo	road
ɛ́ɛrpɔ̀rt	airport

216

sa	to heal, cure
sa	to dance; dip
sã	to lie along
sa, saá	so, thus, in that manner
nsá	hand
nsá	palm wine, alcoholic beverage
ansá	first, at first, meanwhile
ansá na	be before (in time)
ɔsáfɔɔ (pl. a-)	dancer
safõwá, sáfé (pl. n-)	key
samĩná (samĩná)	soap
sãñ	to return, send back
sãñ ákò	to return
sãñ ábà	personally
osáni (pl. asáfɔɔ)	warrior
nsãnõm	drinking, wine-drinking
sę	to day, tell, speak about
sɛ	if, when, whenever; thus, so; in order that, in order to
sɛɛ ɔcɛ́	it is necessary, one must
sɛɛ	to use up, spend; destroy, mar, ruin
sɛ́ɛ́	as like; that (in introducing subordinate
sɛ́ɛ́ ... anãa	if, if, whether
asę, asę́ę́	bottom; down, under; sense meaning
sęgaréétę, sę́gàrɛtɛ	cigarette
osę́káñ (sękáñ) (pl. a-)	knife, razor
asɛm (ásɛm) (pl. n-)	word, saying, story, talk
té ... asɛm	to obey
sempɔá	sixpence
sɛñ	to surpass, pass, excel; more than, than
sɛñ	what, how
sęrá	to visit; smear, grease

217

sẹradẹɛ	fat, grease
ɔsẹram	moon, month
sẹrɛ	to pardon (me), excuse (me), interrupt an angered or off offended person
ɛsẹrɛ (sẹrɛ)	grass
séesei	until now, as yet, still
séesei áà or séesei ára	just, even, ever; the very
sı	to stand, be fixed in upright
sı	position, to put, place, or fix in upright position
sısı	to to stand about
ensíà	six
esıánẹ	because, on account of
sıé	to save, keep
sıésie	to repair, fix, arrange, prepare
sıká	money
sıkákọrá	money-saving, to save money
sıkakọrabẹa	bank, safe, place to keep money
sıkakọrabẹadáñ	bank, bank building
sımmá	minute
esıń (pl. ạsıṇsıń)	part, piece, fragment, remnant
sınıiko	going to the movies, to go to the movies, movie-going
sıñsıń	to cut, carve, sharpe, peel
sırẹṇ	shilling
sısı	to cheat
sísı	a bear
sọ	to catch, seize, take hold of
sɔ	to drip; kindle; try; seal
sɔ ạní	to please, satisfy
sọa	to carry on the head
ɛsọ	the upper part or surface of; on, upon, over, above
ńsọ	also, too

sɔ̃	to be by, large, fat
ɔsófɔọ (pl. a-)	preacher, minister, priest
ɛnsɔ́n̩	seven
sọnọ	to differ, be different
ɛsɔ́nọ	elephant
sorɛ́, sɔ̃m	to be careful about; worship, adore
asórɛ	church service, devotional meeting
ɔsɔ́rọ̀	top, upper part; above, over
n̩sọsọ	also, else
sótehyɛ̀n	station
sɔ́tɔɔ̀	store
suą	to be small, few
osukóm, nsukóm	thirst
sṹą̀	to study, learn, follow the example of
ąsubontɛ́n, asútẹn (pl. n-)	river, stream
ąsubúrà (ą́subúra) (pl. n-)	a well
sukúù	school, school building
sukúùdắn	school building
sukúùní (pl. -fọ̀ọ̀)	student, pupil
nsúo, nsú	water, rain
nsúoąnɔ̃	edge of water, riverbank, lakeside
taa	to chase, pursue
/taa/ plus verb	'to do often'
ataadẹ́ɛ̀ (táádẹ̀ɛ̀) (pl. n-)	clothes, dress, clothes tailored to fit the shape of the body
táẹ̀	tire; necktie
ąksíì	taxi
ąkú, ąkufɛ́	sixpence
ntãmɛ́, ntɔ̃mɛ́	clothes, dress, african dress, wrap-around clothes not tailored to fit the shape of the body

219

tánkę	tank
tę	to perceive, feel, hear; live, dwell; speak a language
tę séέ	to be the same as, be in the same condition or position as
tēe	straight
tékętę	ticket
tèela	tailor
tɛlęfóṅ	telephone
ntέm	haste, swiftness, fast, quick; early, soon
téntēñ	long, high, tall
tęrá, tęná	to sit, live, stay
bɛtęrá	to come, sit down; settle, take up a habitation
tęrá asę	to sit down
tęréṅ	train
etí, etírı (pl. ą-)	head
tıé	to hear, listen
tíìm	team
tɔ	to buy
tɔ	to drop, fall, sink, rain
tǫ	to lay, put; cast, throw; apply to, lay on
tǫ ... mú	to close, lock, shut
tǫ ... ba	to elect, choose, to make a deposit
tǫ ... asę	pay something down
toá	to join, connect, bring together, string; follow, continue
tóṅ	to sell
tǫró, tęró	threepence
tu	to leave, depart; fly; dig, farm, mine
tu kwáñ	to travel, take a trip
tuą	to pay, repay, fill up, replace
tuą	to stick at or in, be stuck at or in

tumí	to be able, can; to be well-versed in, to have permission
tuntum	black; dark shades of blue, green, brown, gray, or tan; very dark red
twạ	to cut, cut up; cross, pass by
twạ asẹ	to draw a line under
twɛn	to wait, wait for, expect
Twíì	the Twi language
ávẹ̀nu	avenue
vísà	visa
wahyẹmán	washerman, launderer
warẹ	to marry, get married
warẹ	to be tall, long
wákyẹ̀	watch
wɔ	to be at; have, own
wɔ, wɔn, wɔn nó	they, their, them
wọ, wu, w-	you, your (sg.)
wọ	to beget, give birth to
awɔ́	cold
awɔ́fọọ, awɔ́fọnǒm	parents
ɛnwotwẹ́	eight
wu	to die
Wúkuoda	Wednesday
owúrà (wúrà) (pl. owúrànǒm)	sir, mister, gentleman
wěí	this, these, that, those
ñ̃wẹnẹ	bitter

221

wĕ̞rɛ	mind, memory; the seat of the emotions
wĕ̞rɛ fı(rı)	to forget
wĭ̞á	to steal
ewĭ̞á, ạwĭ̞á	sunshine; noon, late, early afternoon
ewĭ̞áạdùạnę	lunch, noon meal
ewĭ̞á mũ ạduạné	noon meal
wĭé	to finish, complete
owĭgyınaę̞	afternoon
ewĭ̞m	air, weather, atmosphere
ewĭ̞mhyɛ̃ñ, ewĭmũhyɛ̃ñ	airplane
ñwĭ̞nı̂	to be cold (weather)
ạñwŭmmę́rę	evening, in the evening
ạñwŭmmę́rȩạdùạné	supper, evening meal
ạñwŭmmedùạné	supper

ɛyá	pain, ache; grief, distress
yaa	a response to greetings
yám	to grind
yã̞m̌	to insides of the body
yarȩ̞	to be ill, sick
yarȩ̞ɛ (yárȩ̞ɛ) (pl. ñ-)	sickness, disease
kookóò yarȩ̞ɛ	swollen, shoot disease
ayarȩ́fọọ	patient, sick person, invalid
ayarȩ́fọọ hwɛ́fọọ (pl. ñ-)	nurse
ayarȩhwɛ́fọọ (pl. ñ-)	nurse
ayaresábȩ̞a (pl. ñ-)	hospital
ɔyarȩsáfọ́ɔ	physician, doctor
ɔyarȩsą́nı	physician, doctor
Yáwòda, Yáwǫ̀oda	Thursday
yɛ	to be, exist
ɛy(ɛ) áà	usually
yɛ́	to be good, all right

222

yɛ́	to do, make
yɛ, yɛn	we, our, us
yɛn	to breed, nurse, raise animals
ɔyérɛ (pl. -nõm)	wife, wife's sister
yɪ	to take away, remove; shave, cut the hair
eyɪ́	this, these
yɪyé	good, repaired, mended
yɔ́	to do, make
yɔɔ	yes, O.K., I will comply, I'm listening

PROPER NAMES

Ábɛnaa	Abenaa, a fimale born on Tuesday
Bonsu	Bonsu, a proper name
Adwɔ̂a	Adwoa, a female born on Monday
Afuá	Afua, a female born on Friday
Ghánà	Ghana
Juáasɔ	city of Juaaso
Kégyetia	the city of Kegyetia, a certain road junction to this city
Nkɛrã̃	the city of Accra; the Gã language
Kíñswei	Kingsway store
Kofí	Kofi, a male born on Friday
Koforídua	the city of Koforidua
Ạkósua	Akosua, a female born on Sunday
Ạkúá	Akua, a female born on Wednesday
Kumásɛ	the city of Kumasi
Kwabɛná	Kwabena, a male born on Tuesday
Kwadwɔ́	Kwadwo, a male born on Monday
Kwakú	Kwaku, a male born on Wednesday
Kwamɛ́	Kwame, a male born on Saturday
Kwasí	Kwasi, a male born on Sunday

Ámma	Amma, a female born on Saturday
Omáńñhyiàmúdáñ	House of Parliament
Ménsàh	Mensah, a proper name
Amérẹ̀ka	America
Mpráẹ̀sọ	city of Mpraeso
Asantẹ	Ashanti, name of region and tribe; personal name
Asantẹhẹ́nẹ	the King of Ashanti
Asantẹhẹ́nẹfiẹ́	Asantehene's palace or house
Asantẹwa	Asantewa, a proper name
Nsawam	the city of Nsawam
Sɪká̰a̰guạ Kofí	The Golden Stool, the throne of the Asantehene
Esíremũ	the grasslands in the north of Ghana
Esɪremũfọ́ɔ̀	the inhabitants of grasslands of northern Ghana
Atá	ata, proper name of a male twin
Ataá	Ataa, proper name of a female twin
Tạ́kòrạdí	the city of Takoradi
Tamalẹ	the city of Tamale
Antwɪ	Antwi, a proper name
Owúsù	Owusu, a proper name
Yạá	Yaa, a female born on Thursday
Yaw	Yaw, a male born on Thursday
Yéndɪ̀	city of Yendi